74-76

Uses symbol

JEREMIAH

By Daniel Berrigan

Prose

The Bride: Essays in the Church
The Bow in the Clouds
Consequences, Truth and
Love, Love at the End
They Call Us Dead Men
Night Flight to Hanoi
No Bars to Manhood
The Dark Night of Resistance
America Is Hard to Find
The Geography of Faith (with Robert Coles)
Absurd Convictions, Modest Hopes (with Lee Lockwood)
Jesus Christ
Lights On in the House of the Dead
The Raft Is Not the Shore (with Thich Nhat Hanh)
A Book of Parables
Uncommon Prayer: A Book of Psalms
Beside the Sea of Glass: The Song of the Lamb
The Words Our Savior Taught Us
The Discipline of the Mountain
We Die before We Live
Portraits: Of Those I Love
Ten Commandments for the Long Haul
Nightmare of God
Steadfastness of the Saints
The Mission
To Live in Peace: Autobiography
A Berrigan Reader
Stations (with Margaret Parker)
Sorrow Built a Bridge
Whereon to Stand (Acts of Apostles)
Minor Prophets, Major Themes
Isaiah: Spirit of Courage, Gift of Tears
Ezekiel: Vision in the Dust
Jeremiah: The World, the Wound of God
Daniel: Under Siege of the Holy

Poetry

Time without Number
Encounters
The World for Wedding Ring
No One Walks Waters
False Gods, Real Men
Trial Poems (with Tom Lewis)
Prison Poems

Selected & New Poems
May All Creatures Live
Block Island
Jubilee
Tulips in the Prison Yard
Homage (to G.M. Hopkins)
And the Risen Bread

Drama

The Trial of the Catonsville Nine

JEREMIAH

The World,
the Wound of God

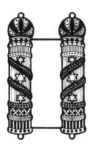

Daniel Berrigan

FORTRESS PRESS
MINNEAPOLIS

JEREMIAH
The World, The Wound of God

Scripture quotations from the New Revised Standard Version of the Bible are copyright © 1989 by the Division of Christian Education of the National Council of Churches of Christ in the United States of America and are used by permission.

Cover and book design by Joseph Bonyata
Woodcuts of Jeremiah and Daniel Berrigan by Robert McGovern

"Veni Creator" by Czeslaw Milosz from Collected Poems, Ecco Press, 1988. Reprinted with permission.

Library of Congress Cataloging-in-Publication Data

Berrigan, Daniel.
    Jeremiah : the world, the wound of God / Daniel Berrigan.
        p. cm.
    Includes bibliographical references.
    ISBN 0-8006-3138-2 (alk. paper)
    1. Bible. O.T. Jeremiah – Commentaries. I. Title.
BS1525.3.B47 1999
224'.207 – dc21   98-22712

The paper used in this publication meets the minimum requirements of American National Standard for Information Sciences—Permanence of Paper for Printed Library Materials, ANSI Z329.48-1984.

Manufactured in the U.S.A.   AF 1-3138

03   02   01   00   99   1   2   3   4   5   6   7   8   9   10

In loving memory
Frederic O'Connor, S.J.
friend, mentor

Contents

Preface

begin with a poem, which I dedicate with all my heart to the mysterious "one man" summoned by the poet:

Come Holy Spirit,
bending or not bending the grasses,
appearing or not above our heads in a tongue of flame,
   at hay harvest or when they plough in the orchards or when
     snow
covers crippled firs in the Sierra Nevada.
  I am only a man; I need visible signs.
I tire easily, building the stairway of abstraction.
Many a time I asked, you know it well, that the statue in church
lift its hand, only once, just once, for me.
But I understand that signs must be human,
therefore call one man, anywhere on earth,
not me—after all I have some decency—
and allow me, when I look at him, to marvel at you.

                                       —*Czeslaw Milosz*

For me, for many years, Jeremiah has been that one man.

❖

My thesis is simple and, I trust, audacious: each of the prophets, in the present instance Jeremiah, is an "other" of Yahweh.

As God's compassionate and clairvoyant and inclusive image, each prophet strives for a divine (which is to say, truly human) breakthrough in the human tribe. Lacerating, intemperate, relentless, the prophets raise the question again and again, in images furious and glorious, poetic and demanding: What is a human being?

We are unready for God; we are hardly more ready for one another.

And yet, and yet...Through the prophets, Yahweh strives mightily for a breakthrough on the human landscape of history, to bring light to our unenlightened human tribe, to speak the truth, unwelcome as it is, of who we are, who we are called to become: friends, sisters, brothers of one another.

This is a tough proposition that goes against the odds of our history, our wars, injustice, and greed, our idolatries. Again and again, these venturesome spirits, the prophets, are warned of the odds: strive as they may, no one—from top to bottom of the social structure, "kings, prophets, priests, people"—will hear; they will turn in despisal from the message of Yahweh.

Worse and worse the warning goes: scorn and obloquy will be the lot of the truth-teller. Frequently the authorities of temple and state will unite against the prophet, invoking the "law of the land." And when the iniquitous law allows it (or even when it does not), the authorities will seek a capital sentence.

Jesus stands in this line of these hapless heroes. Willy-nilly, the afflictions of the prophets are his own. He will echo, some five or six centuries later, the awful word of Yahweh addressed to Jeremiah.

1
The Burden of Awful Events (1:1–19)

The word of Yahweh to Jeremiah is altogether ominous: you will speak, and no one will hearken. Inhibited from birth they are, stalled in a false tradition, morally deaf, dumb, and blind. Insist as you will on a summons from Yahweh to works of justice and compassion; persevere, intercede, and risk all—the response will be indifference, even hatred.

Jeremiah, Isaiah, Ezekiel, and the other great ones press on through a trackless thicket of adverse will. Nothing, or very little, changes. And, despite all, they are never won over to the world's ways, never—short of death—put to silence.

For all their moral greatness, we shall not make of the prophets a species of moral superhumans. True, awful events daunt, discourage, and dishearten. Terrible misfortune and loss befall Jeremiah, Hosea, Daniel, and Isaiah. Suffering is the price exacted of them in their quest for a fuller and deeper humanity—for others, but for themselves first of all. This realization lurks there, between the lines. The great ones admit to it. And someone, against all the odds of Yahweh's prediction to the contrary, nonetheless hearkens to the word and records it. We are left with that record and with its implication for ourselves: What price the human?

They give us one price: to perish, and to have the record of your life and death set down by another. This at best. At worst, to have no record at all. To perish in memory also. That you ever lived. This is the threat.

The Choice before Us: Repentance or Ruin (1:1–3)

"The Lord spoke to Jeremiah...and spoke again...and spoke to him many times."

What a claim! Such assurance: that "take it or leave it," the word of Yahweh—undeviating, polemical—will thunder away for more than forty years!

Who, we ask, was this daring one? He was the worthy, even surpassing, soul brother of the likes of Zephaniah, Habakkuk, Nahum, and Ezekiel. All bear a similar burden of awful events, the downfall of a proud people, exile, and humiliation.

As for Jeremiah, he sees that catastrophe is imminent, is bound to be. Again and again, with the persistence of a clairvoyant or a madman, he shouts the threatening word—repentance or ruin. And inevitably the shout is lost in contrary winds.

It falls on our ears as well, brief, laconic, the bad news that at length came true.

For years, no one took heed. Indeed, who at any period is inclined to take heed of such news as he uttered, who to take it seriously? They turned away, fed up and angered.

All sorts of expediencies are at hand for those who choose not to hear. This naysayer must actually want the worst to occur! He must be guilty of concocting his own brand of bad news, guilty by presumption of ill will, malice, envy, whatever. Like Discord at the king's banquet, he cannot bear that people should prosper. Darkness is his element. And then the last extreme: let the law be invoked against this malefactoring manufacturer of our darkness.

Thus we may with impunity persecute the messenger.

Nonetheless, the awful event Jeremiah warned of is finally at hand; the prophet of doom survives to witness it: "And in the fifth month of that year (the eleventh of the reign of Zedekiah),...the people of Jerusalem were taken into exile."

It was the third roundup of Jeremiah's lifetime. Ten thousand Jerusalemites, we are told, including the royal family, artisans, and nobles, were driven down a road of tears into Babylon. And a puppet is set over those who linger on in the holy city, destroyed and sacked. The national humiliation is complete.

The Choice of Yahweh Falls on Jeremiah (1:4–10)

1:4–5 Now the word of the Lord came to me saying,

> "Before I formed you in the womb I knew you,
> and before you were born I consecrated you;
> I appointed you a prophet to the nations."

There are heavy overtones here of other momentous "choices" on the part of Yahweh and of other heroic types: Moses, Ezekiel, and especially the "suffering servant" of Isaiah. The bearer of the word, it is implied, is foreordained as such. In a sense, the vocation lies outside choice, out of human hands.

What a predicament; what a harsh announcement! It falls, a bolt from the blue: "Before I formed you,...before you were born,...I appointed you."

Does the choice preordain the chosen to joy or sorrow, or both?

Such a word from the Most High, one is tempted to say, were better left unspoken until the point of death, a kind of consolation prize in one's last moments—or perhaps an emollient word offered to survivors. Then it could be borne! But to hear it uttered in one's youth—a word determinant of the entire future? The hundredweight of that!

Jeremiah can only protest: "I don't know how to speak; I am too young." Does he protest too much, as some have claimed? No matter his age, the sense goes deeper. Who, at any stage of life, issued such a summons, would not feel callow, inept, a stutterer?

Suddenly everyone in the world seems more qualified, more gifted, superior, wiser, more apt to win the divine pleasure. Only look about you, young Jeremiah. There are in Jerusalem divines and nobles, savants and saints, priests, elders, prophets—each and all planted in a fruitful soil. There is wisdom aplenty, access to the powerful, instructions handed down with assurance, law, order, honorable service in temple and court. And in face of this ample wit and wisdom, you are the chosen? Yahweh speaking to you? All these others passed over, redundant, of lesser moment?

1:9. It will go on and on, this astonishing story, the powerless nobody and his encounter with the Absolute: "He touched my lips,... 'I will be with you, to protect you.'" Thus in emulation, with the touch of the Holy One upon his flesh, the story of Jeremiah echoes the story of Moses and the other great ones, the foundation blocks of this people's history.

"I will be with you." From beginning to end of scripture, the echo never dies. The first promise and the last. With daring we lift the promise from the page; we claim it for ourselves.

God with us—we know so little of what the promise might mean in practice, what gift it implies, even what form it takes. God, we are told, stands with the poor, the victims, those buried deep at the base of the human pyramid—and with the friends and champions of these. Still, for all that, the history is somber; victims go on being victimized; the best so often go under.

While time lasts, the promise must be taken as ambiguous, dark, all but impenetrable to the logical mind. In this wise: if the power of the Most High is "with us," how comes it that such power so often takes the form of—powerlessness? We look to the martyrs, we hear their outcry.

Perhaps a measure of light dawns when we open the book of Jeremiah.

If the promise bears a crucial weight in one thus assured, if the word of Yahweh is accepted as a premise on which a great spirit proceeds to build a life, to risk all—What weight might the same words exert on us? Less heedless, we will read as we run, and ponder much.

My sense at the outset of the book is that the promise is one matter, the shape of a given life, another. Will the promise shape the life? It all depends. As to Jeremiah, the promise seems meaningless. Would he fare differently, for better, for worse, had it not been uttered? As posed, the question itself is meaningless.

Rightly understood, the promise touches on imponderables.

I venture that the meaning and measure of the promise are clarified in pondering the book itself—taking careful note of Jeremiah's reaction to the atrocious suffering that befalls him. Then the gift shines, the promise holds firm—moral coherence, consistency of word and behavior, undeviating patience, faith and trust though the skies fall.

No one of us has seen the promise vindicated in the lives that beckon us on, over a long, often bitter, haul. Friends keep at unpromising labors; or harder by far, at peaceable confrontations with death-dealing law, ventures that earn only contempt and punishment. We take note of their noble detachment—from successful outcome, self-justification, honor, wealth, the credit of a great name.

This in virtue of the promise.

The hearts of such are fixed elsewhere than in the cultural wasteland. Thus they see good work through to the end, quite simply for its own sake: for its goodness, its human substance, its serviceability and good sense—its being "for others."

All in virtue of the promise.

Jeremiah, yes. And as to ourselves, we shall see.

> 1:10 See, today I give you authority
> over nations and kingdoms
> to uproot and to pull down,
> to destroy and to overthrow,
> to build and to plant.

Jeremiah and Isaiah—the authority is given to them to make the breakthrough to "the nations," to end tribal religion, or, at the least, to make a beginning of the end. The credential is the human itself: all are called, welcomed, included.

The God of Jeremiah, and the God of Isaiah as well, is hereby credited with expanding our vision, high and wide, wide as the world, long as the centuries—so far as to touch, perhaps to transform, ourselves.

The instruction as to behavior and attitude begins with a "no." This will be a capital point throughout the book. The word is uttered in face of what has been acceptable, what is hereby superseded. And a "yes" follows, a summons to what is not yet, but is to be.

The "yes" of Yahweh with respect to ourselves is thus tempered, qualified, with a "no" to our history of crime, war, bloodletting, greed, racism, sexism, injustice of every sort.

A "no," then a "yes." Taken together, the two imply forgiveness, restoration, healing. They take into account ourselves, an ambiguous tribe to whom has befallen—the Fall. The "no" casts its shadow, as does our awful story, truthfully understood, truthfully told. The "yes" rightly comes—afterward. A dawn.

And yet we know that too much stands in the way of a definitive, final, loving "yes"; moral debris clogs and impedes the soul's arteries—crime, death-dealing, war; all that our eyes must see with appalling, and suffer under; the folly and fury of the times; a "meantime" granted the rage of the nations—including our own.

Underscored here is—empires, their woes certainly. And their (possible) weal?

Youthful Jeremiah, calm and forthright, is vested like a new priest with a divine sanction: "Today I give you authority over nations and kingdoms." Nothing quite so explicit, we note, was conferred on Isaiah. Here authority is conferred, and by word of Yahweh. Authority: "the power or right to take command, enforce obedience, take action, or make final decisions."

One senses the public reaction, the anomaly, the derision to follow, the heavy hand come down: "I give you authority over... "?

Let us be, as they say, realistic.

If any quality is common to "the nations," it is the assumption—mortised into the great building blocks of empire, of Supreme Courts and White Houses and Congresses and Pentagons, of armies and navies and marines and nuclear weapons—that this supreme entity, bristling with power and suffused with a sense of glory, is an authority unto itself, is beholden to no other principality, no other nation, no UN, no world court, no international law, no Bible, no conscientious objector.

It is self-enclosed, self-justifying, breathing fire abroad, hermetic, proudly enthroned, sufficient unto itself. A perfectly functioning dominion. From every point of view a "complete environment."

And from a certain point of view (that of the inheritors and achievers and tycoons and judges and politicians and...), what more could be sought from this magniloquent authority? The emoluments, the abounding goods and services, the access to honor and riches—all are for the taking.

As to those others, the poor, the homeless, the stricken veterans of Vietnam and the Gulf slaughter, those excluded from medical care by reason of poverty, what is one to say? And as for the children:

> Of the 57 million of these under 15 years of age... more than 14 million are living below the official poverty level. The United States ranks below Iran and Romania in the percentage of low-birth-rate babies. One of every 6 children is a stepchild; half a million make their "homes" in residential treatment centers and group and foster homes. More children and adolescents in the US die from suicide than from the following combined: cancer, AIDS, birth defect, influenza, heart disease, and pneumonia. And each day, at least one million "latchkey children" go home to where there is a gun. (James Hillman, *The Soul's Guide* [New York: Random House, 1996])

The empire desperately requires a Jeremiah; this is the first fact. What other access to the truth of national behavior, of wars and spoliations, of greed and injustice, can the nation look to?

Perhaps its leaders can turn to counselors, wise ones, princes, diplomats, academics? The prophets are unimpressed. The truth evades such skills as they proffer. We read repeatedly in Daniel, Isaiah, Jeremiah, how the wisdom of the wise fails them. How the great ones, "advised" by such, flounder about in confusion of spirit, face off across uneasy borders, sign and violate pacts with equal aplomb, wage wars relentlessly.

The prophets, on the other hand, speak up in ways that are profoundly dislocating to conventional wisdom and polity. Freedom gives them voice; they have nothing to gain, nothing to lose. They come on abruptly, great refusers and carpers and tellers of unwelcome truths. Self-assured, strangers to doubt and second thoughts (not invariably, at least not Jeremiah, as we shall see!).

They are sent "to the nations." To tell the truth. To stand by the truth they speak. This is the stuff of tragedy, inevitably.

What of the response? A dark logic is at work in the principalities; it is ironbound: the nations reject their prophets.

When we give serious thought to it, a conclusion forces itself: How could that work of such as Jeremiah be integrated, rest in peace with the imperial adventurings of his time? No: he was sent "...to uproot and pull down, to destroy and to overthrow...."

The executive, judicial, deliberative principalities, the vast weaponries, the mailed imperial arm stretching across the world—these to be brought down, destroyed, overthrown?

Yahweh of Jeremiah, are you approving, nay commanding, revolution, subversion?

These last are overheated, overused terms.

Let us take a gentler tack. The above-mentioned entities—the "nations" around whose behavior and ideologies the prophets circle, observe, swoop, harassing like harpies—take to themselves an assumption of life-and-death power, whether in the world at large or within their own borders.

This claim and clutch fell harshly on the people of Jeremiah's time.

A like hundredweight falls today on the people of Jesus.

A great net is cast far and wide: death rows and abortion centers multiply; youths are mustered to kill and die on command; a debate rages whether doctors are to be enlisted to "terminate" lives, whether of the unborn or the "guilty" or the expendable ill and aged.

What then of Jeremiah and his like, of Jesus and his? What response?

The hideous claim upon the living must be scotched, despised, denied, derided, rendered null and void. Its henchmen and hangmen, warriors and sycophants, must be stopped in their tracks. Upon its structures and vile "properties"—armies and courts and jails and death rows, the Pentagon, the think tanks and weapons labs—judgment must fall like a thunderbolt. These are to be uprooted and pulled down, destroyed and overthrown.

In somewhat this wise the charge given to Jeremiah is to be verified time and again—humble and assailed as the effort is bound to be.

Again and again there occurs what is called civil disobedience (which we know as divine obedience) at this or that imperial plague spot. At the Pentagon, the war labs, the naval installations, the air force runways, on bombers and naval craft, blood is poured, symbolic hammers are raised and lowered upon the weaponry.

Thus the structures of death are unmasked and discredited. The truth is once more given place—a small place indeed, but disruptive of the despotism of the Big Lie.

No part in the regimen of death, no incense before idols!

This is the word of the Lord, as spoken to Jeremiah—and to ourselves.

Despite All, "I Will Be with You" (1:11–19)

Without further ado, a storm gathers, dire events are underway.

Verses 11 to 19 are an emotional melee. Words tumble out; they bespeak visions, warnings, social and military chaos to come. And interjected is an urgent, even harsh, message to Jeremiah himself. An hour is shortly to arrive when courage alone will count; everyone will stand against him. A curious threat too: "Do not be afraid of them now, or I will make you even more afraid when you are with them" (1:17).

A lonely vocation is his: "Everyone in the land, kings,…officials, priests, and the people, will be against you." And what or who is to sustain him in face of such massive opposition? "Today I am giving you strength to resist them." Today, even before the crisis arises.

For Jeremiah, the outcome is assured from the start, even as, in an awful sense, the outcome for his people is also assured. The word of Yahweh must stand alone, on its own merit.

The word in all its integrity, be it understood, is one thing—its reception quite another. So must the speaker of the word stand and withstand, more often than not, alone, a guardian, a lonely sentinel of the truth. Regardless of outcome.

Such understanding, entering the soul's fiber and weaving it anew, gives rise to marvelous images of strength. Jeremiah "will be like a fortified city, an iron pillar, and a bronze wall." Which is to say: as possessor of the truth, possessed by the truth, your strength surpasses that of all the others—"kings,... officials, priests, and the people." A bit much, somewhat inhuman?

At the start, two visions are granted; neither is reassuring. From the north, ruin awaits, war, defeat, exile. And a question arises: Are the visions granted for Jeremiah alone or for the sake of his people? Are we perhaps included, who come after?

So, a time warp.

The dire events prophesied come to pass. The outcome is a matter of history. So is its cause: inattention and contempt paid to a warning that might have averted tragedy.

Once there was time, it is implied: time for conversion, time to grant place to the truth. But no one hearkened.

Why hearken? The kingdom of Judah was manifestly prospering, no cloud obscured the horizon. Prosperity stood firm as a bronze stele. Not to be wondered that the word of Jeremiah seemed a mere confabulation.

Another impediment, grave, greater by far than the inattentive politics of affluence, stood in the way: "They have abandoned Me,... have made idols and worshiped them."

That famous stele; it bore the image of a golden calf. Here was the nub of the matter, and more: social commentary with a vengeance.

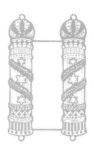

2
Idolatry Omnipresent, Yahweh Contemned (2:1–4:31)

History, a Sorry Record (2:1–37)

History yes, a witness:

2:2–26 For the prosecution!
In your youth, fidelity stood firm,
afterward—you fell away.

To the sorry record
I add not a word—
plucked from slavery,
cozened, held close,
through deserts uninhabitable,
I spread before your feet
like a fragrant carpet
a land fragrant, unfolding,
flowing with milk and honey, my
benignity and promise!
And all awry, unfair—
the promise polluted, the land
gone in a season
flourishing,
        then repining.

A harrowing of hell!
rulers rebellious
priests reneging
prophets mouthing
the detested name: Ave Baal!

My people, my semblable
my enemy!
Who tames, who reins you in?

Look how you turn and turn
from springs of living water
souls immersed, unslaken
at brackish pools!

2:8. The priests are grown sterile. They no longer ask, "Where is the Lord?" They are obsessed with niceties of personal conduct, reduced to niggardly specialists of the law.

"Knowledge of Yahweh," that precious inheritance and legacy, a wisdom both overriding and penetrating, is all but vanished. (The "all but" is crucial. Its name is Jeremiah.)

The people are parched with thirst; they can discover in the priesthood no source of that precious knowledge. (Hosea spoke the same reproach to the priests [4:4–10], including the "giving over of the Glory [i.e., Yahweh], to idols.")

To this has the priesthood come; it is the slavish acolyte of nothings, idols, confabulations.

2:26–37. A torrent of reproaches erupts from the lips of outraged Yahweh.

Enough has been enough, and too much. The wild venture of creation, that breathtaking chance taken on freedom, on love, presupposed as its glory an attentive people, faithful to the holy compact.

Thus at the genesis a munificent wager was cast by Yahweh, in favor of humankind. And (at least as here recorded), the wager was lost.

Both parties to the covenant lost. One Party reckons its loss in infinite bitterness, as recorded by Jeremiah. And the "other party"? It takes no account of its dolorous loss; in a most vulgar sense, it prospers. For now.

This is how Yahweh sees the world: a nest befouled with discontent; a people feverish, morally confused, directionless, aping this imperial neighbor and that, worshipful of this god and that; a people who turn and twist like the heathen, in dark corridors of worldly power and might.

And Yahweh is probing, mourning, raging, reproving, reminding—missing nothing.

What do they seek? What are they in quest of? We have no recorded response.

Jeremiah, for his part, is uninterested in a response. To him, faithful, intent, and morally lucid, there can be no response worth recording.

According to the oracle, the people are to be judged and condemned; even in absentia. There is no defense; they are simply pushed off the page.

Notably, we have here a different method than that of the Gospels. There, whatever the vigor of *parti pris* or the presumed omniscience of the scribe, invariably a place and a hearing are granted to the adversaries. The secular and religious establishment—priests, Sanhedrin, Pharisees, Sadducees, Pilate, Herod—all walk the pages, invoke the law, at some length justify themselves, speak their version of events.

Here, matters are more sternly dealt with. Yahweh offers only the slightest hint that a hearing (of sorts) is to be granted the delinquent people (2:34–35).

And even then, the defense presented is no more than hearsay. Its argument reaches us at a second remove, from the mouth of the offended party: "In spite of all this, you say: 'I am innocent; surely Yahweh is no longer angry with me.'"

The procedure strikingly resembles that in vogue among Eastern potentates.

But a question arises: Does the bias of the method weaken the charges adduced? Were "equal time" granted the defense, would the procedure bring a larger measure of truth to bear? Or is the notion of a "defense" no more than a distraction, an attempted evasion of the truth of the situation—the moral impasse devastatingly laid bare in the pages of Jeremiah? (An impasse, must one not underscore it, lamentably verifiable in every time and locale—which is to say, our Fall from grace?)

Part of us would object: the people accused are granted no chance of answering the accusations. Surely a "democratic process" would assure greater chance of a just outcome! And part of us is inclined to admit: there is no defense.

The notion that the charge could be groundless lies somewhere between delusion and distraction. The truth is that Jeremiah's Yahweh has laid bare in awful image after image—simply the human predicament, our Fall from grace. Our sole recourse, our feeble strength, such as it is?—admission of guilt.

This is the way the Fall from grace befalls a later generation, our own. Day after day, the truth of the charge of Yahweh is verified in our midst. Slaughter of the innocent is followed by ruinous sanctions against the Iraqis; the people of Cuba are likewise punished; the earth is wasted with nuclear residue; contempt for one another is rife; the poor are victimized and blamed.

Why the slippery evasions? Why not confess and have done with it?

This is admission—we the people, then and now, are guilty. We renege on the covenant. The charges brought in the indictment of 700 BCE are verifiable among us, in this, our bloodshot century. We too run after other gods, idols that we "made for ourselves." We too proclaim, in the telling image of verse 27, that "a tree is our father and a rock our mother." We too have said in effect: stocks and stones are our gods (nukes have begotten us, violence suckled us).

(We are told that in the fertility cults the "wooden post" denoted the female principle, and the "stone pillar" the male. And Jeremiah heaps derision on these symbols of default, weirdly reversing their sexual innuendo.)

We too have ignored (when we have not capitally punished) the prophets. We have "as many gods as we have cities." We declare in actions that speak loud, "We will do as we please,...will never come back to you." And this, even as our "clothes are stained with the blood of the poor and innocent...." (It is worth noting, too, that when sins of sexual depravity are mentioned, as in verse 33 and passim in the prophets, they lead beyond themselves as symbols of idolatry.)

The God Who Weeps, Rejected (3:1–25)

3:1-3 If a man divorces his wife
and she goes from him
and becomes another man's wife,
will he return to her?
Would not such a land be greatly polluted?
You have played the whore with many lovers;
and would you return to me? says the Lord.

Look up to the bare heights, and see!
Where have you not been lain with?
By the waysides you have sat waiting for lovers,
like a nomad in the wilderness.
You have polluted the land
with your whoring and wickedness.
Therefore the showers have been withheld,
and the spring rain has not come;
yet you have the forehead of a whore,
you refuse to be ashamed.

Prostitution again (vv. 1, 2)—and in consequence the defaulting of nature itself (v. 3). That insight, so ancient, is such a scandal, causes such fretting for logical, critical minds!

As I set down these notes in the summer of 1995, we of the East Coast are enduring one of the worst droughts in memory. The stately Hudson River is languishing. A spectacle unseen in my lifetime: from the fountainhead south to the New York islands, miles of algae choke the life of the majestic stream. More: as the water level falls, salt water from the harbor creeps upriver, endangering fresh water for a distance of sixty miles and more.

Scientific attributions of the catastrophe are numerous: snowfall of the previous winter was slight, ocean currents are warming, and so on.

One supposes that scholars agree with reluctance with what might be termed a biblical conclusion here, or at least a conclusion according to Jeremiah. In the book we read of a situation in nature that seems uncomfortably close to our own. There is a drought; as to its cause, God reasons thus: "You have played the whore with many lovers"; "Where have you not been lain with?" And immediately: "Therefore the showers have been withheld, and the spring rain has not come."

Are we to take the text at face value?

In 1995 a blazing summer, and no rains. And then the "prostitution" of the culture of the day, our multiple idolatries of greed and violence.

What to make of the text?

"The Bible habitually generates ambivalence....Characterisation is complex, the motives mixed, the plot riddled with gaps and enigmas, behavior unpredictable, surprises omnipresent, the language packed and playful" (Meir Sternberg, *The Poetics of Biblical Narrative* [Bloomington: Indiana University Press, 1985]).

It is of course easy to dismiss the beginning of Jeremiah 3 and its lyric leap, linking human default and failing nature as cause and effect. It is so primitive, naive, otherworldly, out of line with scientific attributions!

It would be easier, one is tempted to retort, if the text at hand were not so often repeated, were not in fact a constant harping of the Bible. Texts as ancient as Genesis, ignoring our "secondary causes," insist on the seamless web uniting the physical and moral worlds.

Biblically we are being constantly reminded, warned: look to it. It is we who weave or ravel the original fabric of Genesis. And in so doing, weave or ravel our own destiny.

Verses 1 to 18 are one long, ruminating plaint, image after image of the pain of a rejected God. This God, for all his purported "power and might" over creation, including our human tribe, is no one of the sort. The Fall has befallen him also. He is reduced to powerlessness, caught up short. In the world, he is a stranger, an exile, suspect, scorned, unwanted. Or "wanted, for questioning."

In the benighted conduct of this people, the war of myths proceeds apace—Yahweh versus the gods. Who made the world? Who in consequence owns the world? To whom are we responsible?

The gods are secretive; we hear nothing from them; perhaps they have nothing to say. Or perhaps, as Yahweh declares, they are no more than "trees and rocks," figments of distempered imagination and skills gone to rot.

In any case Yahweh refers to them with absolute contempt.

Nonetheless, these gods, God implies, hold on a tight rein the destiny of their worshipers. Consequent to socialized idolatry, a momentous displacement of reality has occurred. The gods, not God, are in command of the world. The members of the pantheon are commonly considered greater beings, more powerful, more bountiful, more giving—they embody in sum a greater measure of the reality associated with the divine, the numinous, than does God.

Obeisance is due them; it is *dignum et justum*. Not him.

Jeremiah, we note, is not here dwelling on the sins of the "nations." To the desolate contrary, the Plague of the Godlings is rampant among the chosen. (Idolatry among the nations is quite taken for granted; it is not at issue.)

Behold the abomination: Judah and Israel have fallen to knee before stocks and stones. They have declared other parenthood than the Creator; declared, in a phrase Yahweh quotes as their own, "A tree is your father and a rock your mother."

Idolatry Omnipresent, Yahweh Contemned (2:1–4:31)   **15**

Each idolater is an "unfaithful woman," "divorced" from Yahweh and turned "prostitute." The terms of abomination yield to "adultery," in turn equated with worship of rocks and trees.

3:11–15. Yahweh's plaint ends. Jeremiah speaks in his own person. Israel is, it appears, reformable; more so than Judah. The words yield to generosity of spirit, as welcome as it is unexpected. The "return" of each is envisioned, with Israel repenting first.

The terms set in verse 13 are instructive: "Admit...guilt...confess...." Then the process of "return" can get underway, with "I will take one from each town and two from each clan and bring you back to Mount Zion" (v. 14).

An instance of the famous "remnant"?

In any case, who are these chosen ones? Are we to summon the story of Daniel and his companions, keeping strict kosher and discipline of prayer among the "nations"? Or perhaps old Tobit and his persistent, lonely fidelity to Torah?

Perhaps the likes of these. The few once chosen, a further promise is offered, a reward.

How speedily, all but preemptively, Yahweh moves! "I will give you rulers who obey me, and they will rule you with wisdom and understanding" (v. 15).

The sequence is not to be missed. It is obedience to Yahweh that results in humane, compassionate, civic governance.

(Obedience, sound governance: an alignment much longed for by those under the heel of inhuman authority.)

(And a further question: What quality of obedience does a predatory authority engender? Servility, ignobility?)

3:16. "Breathtaking" would seem an apt word to describe the moment in verse 16: a stupendous prediction is aired, a momentous foreshadowing of the covenant to come (enlarged on in 31:27ff.). In the shambles of an unpromising, inhuman, necrophilic time, on a horizon darker than darkness, Jeremiah declares it: one day a light will arise.

In time to come, the old "covenant box" will be broken asunder, the tablets of stone cast aside. But what of the covenant to which the ancestors bound themselves—only to break their vows like so much match wood?

The city is destroyed, the Ark broken in pieces, never to be repaired. It is as though Yahweh too has seen the utter uselessness in practice of the ancient law. "They will no longer think about or remember it; they will not even need it; nor will they make another one" (v. 16).

What then is to stand in place of the former law? Do we humans not require moral boundaries and sanctions?

The questions are haunting. And we are offered no answers here. Only this: ever so slightly, Jeremiah's Yahweh opens the door on a vista of hope. We are offered a glimpse, and no more, of a humanity restored. Our own?

Just as quickly the door is closed.

We are left there, at a portal closed. Indeed the door merges with a wall of mute history. History a conundrum, our plight.

One could question, with some reason: Might it not have been to our advantage that the door were never opened?

The subject is left there, a vast question mark—ourselves, our fate, our future. Who are we, who shall we be? Crooked as we are, bowed under the yoke of sin, shall we be raised up, straightened, healed? Shall we one day take the form of an exclamation point, a huzzah, an alleluia—an Easter? "Eye has not seen, nor ear heard. . . . "

We shall know on "that day," but not now.

3:17. The promise hovers there. And the scene shifts, to beloved Jerusalem: "When that time comes, . . . all nations will gather there to worship me." The vision is Isaian, universal.

Always this shift, from utmost realism regarding the "worst of times" (the times we endure as best we might) to another, better time, a time so in contrast with the present as to be all but unimaginable: a "time to come."

So awful the present, so wearying and profitless, is it to be wondered that we fall from hope? In such times, evil seems malignant, persistent, even "natural"—no temporary aberration, but the final shape of things. A different shape, a world of peace and compassion, a welcoming circle large as all humanity—that seems unreal, hallucinatory, a dream to seduce the dreamer.

When will the "on that day" be here, be now? The "time to come" is indefinitely delayed. Nevertheless, despite all, the day nears. It comes closer: in Jesus, in the martyrs of our lifetime. We have seen the dawn of "that day," and rejoice.

3:19–25. Verses 19 to 22: indictment; and verses 23 to 25: response. At long last, it would seem that a different spirit is stirring in hearts that seemed of stone.

Jeremiah has borrowed his text from liturgies of repentance, as did Hosea before him (6:1–6). Those "hilltops" or "heights" (v. 2) where abominations were practiced, now become a scene of relenting and lamentation. And Yahweh seems shaken by the former infidelities, gropes about confounded, in search of images. Within a few verses, we note the mix of metaphors/relationships: "Son,... father,... unfaithful wife... "

Beginning with verse 21, a change of heart is verified—and the theme is enlarged throughout. This is a clue: Baal is named for the first time as "god of shame." Worship of the idol has degraded the people—as well as fueling the anger of Yahweh. And more: the same worship has "made us lose flocks and herds," and, worst of all, "sons and daughters."

The reference is unclear: perhaps the catastrophes occurred in the travail of exile, or after the return, through famine and drought? Or have the sons and daughters been lost, not to death, but to family unity and affection? Did they worship Baal along with the elders, and afterward refuse to join in the common repentance? Or another possibility: perhaps they had remained faithful to Yahweh, at cost of family unity. An intriguing lacuna, with many questions unanswered.

One hesitates to leave the theme of "loss of the young," an event of tragic moment today also. The church loses "sons and daughters," hugely, in neglecting to announce and bless and proffer the pith and marrow of the faith.

A Truth That Reeks with Blood (4:1–31)

The time sequence in chapter 4 is of interest here as elsewhere. Accustomed as we are to a linear "before and after," we are somewhat set off kilter with the disinterest of the prophet in precise narration, event following event. We shortly come to see the point: the prophet is not setting down a book of Kings or Chronicles, or Exodus.

He will refer, almost in passing, to massively important events: invasions, defeats, exile, and return. But the record kept, if such a term is useful, is a matter of heart rather than mind, of resonance and inference rather than logic.

His method might be called musical in the classical sense. A theme is announced, and left largely unexplored. A second and perhaps a third theme follow. Then the variations take over; each theme in turn is played upon again and again, with nuances: detailed, playful, serious, meandering, inviting, awakening.

So in the prophets too, much is left to ourselves, unsaid, inferred through metaphor and simile, prose and poetry. A headlong imprecation followed by a pause, tender, childlike. There are great outpourings of emotion, variations of anger, sin and consequence, mercy and repentance.

4:2. This is one of those "sleeper" texts Jeremiah slips into the book—Shall we say slips all but past us? The sequence is clear, the inference bold. A first and absolute requirement is set down: removal of the idols. In second place, renewal of truth, justice, and righteousness. To these add *hesed* (piety, love, compassion), and we are offered a precious summary of true religion.

Then the conclusion, astonishing on the face of it, yet in close accord with experience. A faithful, worshipful people give this witness before the world: Yahweh is our God. "Then all nations will ask me to bless them, and they will praise me."

The promise is an ancient one, as old as the period of patriarchs (Gen. 12:3; 18:18). Experience verifies both the longing and the blessing, yes. The nations, admit it or not, look to, long for, the witness of believers. (Camus and C. Wright Mills were such "unbelievers" calling us to accounts; in effect: "These Christians, do they believe anything?" God knows, as these writers knew, the world and worldly systems have little to offer of substance or spirit.)

Only let an Oscar Romero or a John XXIII or a Martin Luther King appear on the scene—what hope hangs on the air, what emulation!

And one reflects with shame on the counterwitness also offered. Official church policies, but for their carefully laid veneer of religious rhetoric, much resemble their secular counterparts. Firm lines are drawn; law and order is in the ascendancy; expulsions and exclusions are thunderous on the air; women and gays and the divorced are put down or put to the door.

Thus appears the church one loves: as a cold-hearted officialdom, clinging to power and place. And alas, the "nations" turn elsewhere. The warrant is no longer credible; the authority lacks a human face.

> 4:4 Circumcise your hearts…
> or my anger will burn like fire.…
> It will burn, and there will be no one to put it out.

Moods and moods. Here a fiery interlude. The rawness of the words!

Much more is to be required than a temple renovation, a dusting up, the revival of long neglected prescriptions, and so on—what might be thought of as "liberal reform." To circumcise the heart is another matter entirely; it is a painful, even bloody, business. And yet, once undergone, the surgery brings both intelligence and will—to rebirth.

The anger of Yahweh is combustible. Creation is its tinder. And the "no one" of the text denies any and all exception. "No one to put out" such fires—except Yahweh, who kindled them.

Still, the anger admits of a change of mood. The angry One is also the merciful One, as we are reminded repeatedly. Yahweh has other moods; therefore, we take hope.

Reminded of the divine anger, one is strangely heartened. Perhaps anger is befitting to us also. How frequently in such days, one is all but consumed with anger at the spectacle of a malfunctioning church and state, of blind leaders leading the blind. I ask myself and others (and God): Who could dwell in such a world with open eyes, with even half a heart, and be free of anger?

Much mercy in my heart, an overflow of painful compassion, toward the victims whom I see daily on my street—it seems everywhere in the world. A world that bleeds and groans before my horrified gaze.

So much suffering needlessly, maliciously, blindly imposed. Hopes dashed to ground. Betrayal as a common political coin, tossed in contempt toward the victims. Sanctions, matters of life and death, medicine and food, imposed against children. Refugees stigmatized as alien, unwanted, "illegal" (as though a human could be illegal)—and sent packing.

On the one hand, the wreckers and breakers; on the other, myself—with little of mercy toward them, full more of judgment, of fiery anger, even of cursing. Many times arrested, many times hailed in court, many times an "authority" has pressed hard on me, willy-nilly (more nilly by far than willy!)—"To uproot and to pull down, to destroy and to overthrow."

I hold another image dear, facing as I must the entrenched systems of the world: Jeremiah at the start of his ministry. This is how God sees the prophet, a harsh grace conferred on him: "You will be like a fortified city, an iron pillar, and a bronze wall."

It comes to me with the force of a firestorm, the fire of Yahweh's anger. The great mercy one offers the merciless is not to give up, against odds to go on: to serve those ill of AIDS, to be arrested, often and bootlessly, to offer retreats and teaching, meals, hospitality. And all the while poring over the Bible, taking the word seriously, day after day.

Learn in those pages, and lodge in your heart, anger and mercy both, and the blessing accruing to each:

Injustice has always hit me hard. I suffer along with it....It has always bothered me that human beings can be treated like slaves.

God is my hope—I have little hope in armies, in the powerful, in dogmas or absolute truth....

I began to reflect about the dirty world in which poor people live, about the garbage dumped into the barrios.... Poor people produce very little garbage—it is the powerful who take over the territory of the poor, dumping their garbage.... And in my flesh, I began to feel a connection between this and the destruction of the environment, of the land and of people....

The most important thing Christianity has given me is my inability to conform to the injustice and pain of those who suffer. My faith tells me that the meaning of life is to struggle so that people may live in dignity, so that the earth may fulfill its right to thrive as a living being, housing us in mutual respect....

The bottom line is that we women are not accepting the words of masculine power. This is a huge, qualitative change, and it is paradoxical. Even though we are living right now in one of the most destructive moments ever in our world, inside that destruction huge changes are taking place.

All over the world, small groups of women are saying no to their situations. They are organizing,...demanding respect for our ecosystem, seeking to solve problems through regional solutions that permit a harmonious coexistence with the environment. These initiatives are like a tiny oasis in a desert of destruction.

And it is not just women; it is also...scientists, ecologists, men and women alike....

Twenty years ago, in Latin America, in the United States, you didn't hear anyone talking about change coming through women, theology from women—a theology that comes from the flesh....

Feminist theology is presenting this challenge to liberation theology—the need to relocate the Christian vision of our planet, of humanity, our "cosmovision," within a wider perspective. (Ivone Gebara, silenced by the Vatican)

At 4:5 we begin a long antiphonal passage, all one poem really. Yahweh, Jeremiah, and the people speak. The theme is dour—and no wonder. In a passage reminiscent of Joel, Jeremiah cries out: Let there be a season of mourning and repentance! And he weeps, knowing the disaster even then near, the storm gathering.

He is fearless before fearsome Yahweh (4:10). And a reproach, strange and unwonted in face of the constant threats of Yahweh, arises on his lips: "You have completely deceived the people of Jerusalem! You have said there would be peace, but a sword is at their throats" (4:10). (The Jerome Commentary: "This promise of welfare is said to be Yahweh's, and the present event shows that he lied; however, this allusion is clearly to the preaching of the false prophets [6:14; 14:13–16]." Or so it is said.)

The reproach, as delivered, goes unanswered.

4:13. A great wailing arises, but no change of the heart of God. Yahweh, it is clear (v. 18 and passim), has set his face against a sinfully recusant people. His words are fierce, his intent beyond mistaking. It is he who stirs up the Babylonians to move against Jerusalem.

We would be inclined to put matters differently. In view of the worst, God allows the worst. Wicked behavior invites a disastrous outcome, ineluctably.

4:19–22. Jeremiah is shaken at the dark prospects lurking in the wings of the drama; so is Yahweh shaken (see v. 22). More: the prophet is heartbroken, the suffering to come so shortly upon a people who, all said, are his own!

Do we have here the prevision of Jeremiah, or a dirge composed on the day of disaster itself? We do not know. But in either case, a spirit both valiant and premonitory is overwhelmed by a world witlessly preparing for war, or actually at war.

Another question suggests itself: Would the suffering the prophet endures at the prospect (or actual sight) of defeat have been mitigated if his people were to issue victorious? Is the defeat of one's own people, and violation of legitimate national feeling, the point of the dirge? Or is the teaching far more demanding, a universal condemnation of war itself? Is even "legitimate self-defense" to be regarded as yet another sin, another violation?

Is Yahweh, albeit indirectly, counseling nonviolent resistance (as seems the case in Isaiah, even while the enemy stands at the gates of Jerusalem)?

Here we are left uncertain.

Judah has been invaded (or is about to be invaded) by the cruelest of enemies. Shortly the Southern Kingdom will be swallowed by the gargantuan appetite of Babylon. Nation, temple, Jerusalem the beautiful—all will be obliterated. A caravan of the lost will wind its somber way, under guard, into slavery.

> 4:23–26 I surveyed my land—
> barren, a waste.
> I looked on high—
> a torrent of darkness.
>
> The mountains shake like an ague,
> rock, sway, a molten sea.
> Birds of the air are fled.
> My beloved land a desert.
> Cities, ruins, bare rookeries.
>
> And where, where are my people?
> You, Yahweh, your doing—
> desolation.

On the part of the people, no change of heart occurs. So be it; on the part of Yahweh, no turning back. Thus the impasse, and the rising of cosmic images of primordial chaos, terror, the land denuded. Such images haunt also the pages of Joel, Amos, Zephaniah, Nahum.

War is literally regarded here as the end of the world, identified simply with the "Day of the Lord." The prophets, stricken as they are, are authentic witnesses. A world is coming to closure; the homeland, that "peaceable kingdom," the holy city, self-violated, self-mutilated, is crashing down.

In the prophets, we note that "the world" is never generic; it is one's own world. It is the slow cohering over long time of a culture; friends and family and land and language and dance and song; a world of coherence and beauty, each element infinitely precious, irreplaceable. Thus "the world," a cohesion of beauty and truth and joy, makes sense, wins the heart, becomes one's own—as a dance does, a poem, a work of art. (Especially for the children, that "world" in all its fragility is to be cherished and guarded, a nest in which coherence, truth, and tenderness are honored.)

What then must the assault on Dresden or Coventry or Hiroshima or Hanoi or Baghdad have seemed like, to those who walked innocent into their last hour, or vainly took shelter in cellars and caves, as the bombs crashed down?

Was it not, for countless adults and children, the end of the world?

4:31. This section of the poem ends with the cry of a woman in travail. She is Jerusalem; she is an entire people—and she is one woman and her anguish. She is giving birth to a child, her first; she endures both pain and anticipation. And she cries out. It is no ordinary cry; it breaks the membrane of the metaphor: "Woe is me, for I faint before murderers." Nothing had prepared us for a truth that reeks with blood—and not solely the blood of childbearing.

The pangs of childbirth are one thing; a deadly assault on a woman is another. The first image brings us a certain measure of insight. Then, implies Jeremiah, to attain the truth we must go further: war is at hand, and war is murder.

It is murder most heinous. It is the murder of a woman, a "noncombatant"; and since the child's birth nears, the unborn perishes also.

3
The People Dwell in
Moral Darkness (5:1–31)

The first chapters have stressed religious failings, the dolorous omnipresence of idolatry. Now we enter another form of code violation, that of social sins—a vast arena indeed. In it, one after another, the prophets wrestled with the powers.

Your Eyes Seek Only Truth, Yahweh (5:1–10)

Verses 1 to 6 present a dialogue between Yahweh and Jeremiah. For sake of one person "who does justice, who seeks truth" (or who is "upright, faithful," and forgets not *hesed* [that third in the triad of gifts that define the ideal human])—for sake of this rare spirit, God would save Jerusalem, as he would have saved Sodom (Gen. 18:22).

This one person: Is he not present, we ask, in Jeremiah? Does he not do justice and seek truth? Does he not shine bright amid the darkness? Or is such nobility taken for granted, God meantime seeking another?

"They swear falsely" (v. 2), a common tactic (then and now). That is, they invoke God, but only in furtherance of a shady deal. Thus a spate of sacred smog is released on the air, wonderfully obscuring the truth of the issues at hand.

In the short run, the tactic works well, not merely in the wide world of wheeling and dealing, but in "religious" circles as well. In such a way, those who embody such virtues as justice and truth can be put to the door. And seldom has bad faith worn a more innocent face!

But then in verse 3: "But O Lord, do not your eyes look for the truth?" How beautiful, how telling. The eyes of Yahweh are like the eyes of a child. From a garden of innocence, unclouded with the ambiguities of the life of the fallen, the gaze of the Holy One falls on the world. The eyes of Jeremiah, our truth-teller, are such. His eyes too look on the world—with an innocence hard won, to be sure.

He knows the God of truth; which is to say, he knows that God *is* truth, that the truth is native to Yahweh, is synonymous with the holy name itself.

(One is tempted to add, truth is as native to Yahweh as it is foreign to the human scene.)

As for ourselves and despite all, Jeremiah knows that a capacity for truth is the glory of our humanity; perhaps the first glory of all. To seek the truth—passionately, persistently, and thereby to come on it and announce it in the world—is simply to name ourselves human, and therefore godly.

The truth, as they say, is the first casualty of war.

But what of a "peace time" from which the truth is also banished, equally a stranger? Such times of untruth, which I believe our times to be, require that for sake of the truth—endangered, despised, banished—a hard truth be set down. Truth, we suggest, is by no means native to the "human condition" as we witness it, and endure it, and mourn for its wounding.

Alas for truth. We see instead a culture and climate in which duplicity, betrayal, doublespeak, surreptitious dealing, guile, treachery, and low cunning are the "normal" tools of political intercourse.

The chefs of chicanery proceed to marinate the above admirable qualities in a bland sauce of religious fakery. Thus, for example, "family values" become the sanctified code for a nouveau brand of fascism.

Verses 4 and 5 are puzzling, on the face of it. One longs to know more about the sociological suppositions at work here. Is our Jeremiah, scion of an elitist priestly family, here uncharacteristically disdaining the poor? "They are foolish, they do not know the way of God, the ordinance of the Lord" (v. 4). Even granted the rightness of such a judgment, one is impelled to ask: Is no connection to be drawn between the ignorance of the lowly ones and the blindness of the powerful (among whom must be accounted the priestly caste, as Jeremiah immediately concedes)? If the lowly are redeemed only with difficulty, who is responsible for their plight? If they are to be accounted sheep, where are the shepherds?

Priests talk a priestly jargon; they have favorite formulas at hand. So Jeremiah; he repeats the phrase earlier applied to the lowly. Now the great ones, kings, priests, prophets, are judged "not to know the way of God, the ordinance of the Lord" (v. 5).

Is the irony intentional, or does it escape Jeremiah? Is bad faith here condemned? Are the powerful ones indicted for knowing the truth and turning away from it? Or is a (naive) supposition implied on his part: that these "great ones," knowledgeable in Torah as they are, can with ease be brought to a change of heart? If such be the case, Jeremiah's awakening is rude. "They too with one accord have broken the yoke and burst the bonds."

Worthy of note: the same violent image was never applied to the lowly.

Undeniably the lowly ones dwell in a moral twilight. But they have hardly created it; rather, the moral darkness of the "great ones" overwhelmed them as well. Kings and rulers and counselor and the wealthy are spoken of far differently; they have played violent hob with boundaries anciently set in place—boundaries, moreover, whose guardians and watchmen they were appointed to be. There is betrayal here, and a contemptuous overthrow of tradition.

What and where were the boundaries? Adultery-idolatry is of point. The distinction is left unclear; the one sin would appear to meld with the other, a familiar usage among the prophets, a kind of mutual metaphor.

In verse 6, the wild animals are images of the invaders, as in 2:15 and 4:7.

In verse 10, the outcome of the covenantal lapse is a kind of noble biblical cliché; the land suffers under the disregarding heel of a renegade people. Could it not be that contempt for Yahweh ("they have worshiped gods that are not real") leads inexorably to contempt for creation, its consequent misuse and degradation?

And could not one add—vice versa?

The People Dwell in Moral Darkness (5:1–31)   27

The World Be Our Icon (5:12–19)

Atheism in practice. A shrug, and life goes on. In effect:

5:12–13   We hear a giddy spate of talk, most of it dire,
from these windy ones.
Ruin, invasion, slavery indeed!
But have no fear;
this god, whether real or a confabulation of theirs,
who can know?
In any case, nothing of their wild talk
will come to pass.
If he exists at all, distant he surely is,
uninterested, morally neutral. [cf. Amos 9:10;
   Zeph. 1:12]
One lives therefore as one lives;
let the world be our icon.

Of contempt we have heard much; here the theme arises again. God is contemned, in practice. (Indeed is there a form of contempt for God other than moral malpractice?)

The next step: the prophets must be pulled down from high public regard. Have they been called men of *ruah*, of "the spirit"? The spoliators will turn the word to insult. At long last, we see their god, their Yahweh, for what he is: the confabulation of a handful of enthusiasts; their Yahweh is a decrepit dream, a rumor, a passing wind.

Still, inner unease haunts us.

This matter of Yahweh, whether he exists, who he might be, what demands the covenant places on us—these are not easily disposed of.

Nor is Jeremiah. By no means deflated, the man of *ruah*, a vessel of the spirit—he speaks up again and again (see 5:14–17). Unquenchable! And this, though a wave of socialized contempt has gathered, to silence him and render his message null and void.

But denial has taken a further step: an anathema is issued against Jeremiah. And worse: a practical (and practiced) atheism—denial of the First Prophet of all, Yahweh—is abroad.

Is the message of Jeremiah true? Is it false? All said, the question can by no means be dealt with in the abstract. The clue revolves around moral behavior, visible, public, political. In such choices, whether momentous or quotidian, Yahweh is granted recognition; or is refused it.

The refusal strongly implies that Yahweh is discredited. Thus too with the man of *ruah*.

Doggedly, Jeremiah persists. What was prophesied will come to pass. They are doomed; they have brought the pillars of heaven down—upon themselves.

Verses 18 and 19 are of interest. Possibly a midrash? In the universal darkness, ever so slightly a door comes ajar, a shaft of light appears. It is that slim chance that is granted even to fools and their follies. It is called hope.

Did someone, a later scribe, daringly add the verses, a kind of postscript or footnote—after the fact? (And by no means discrediting the awesome insight of Jeremiah, and the catastrophe that long since descended.)

But still, but still, a gentle caveat: "Even in those days, I will not completely destroy my people." Woe is not all the human condition, though it be very nearly all. Nor is the end yet, though wickedness bring it perilously near.

The Sea Obeys Me, but You Will Not (5:20–31)

5:20–25. The benignity of creation is both fact and metaphor; it shines transparent "in autumn rains and spring rains and…the harvest season each year" (5:24). Occasions for rejoicing and gratitude, rains and seasons are also a metaphor; they lead beyond themselves to the Giver of good things.

Or they should. But often do not. Thus Yahweh: "You never thought to honor me" (5:24). Therefore the drought descends. So close an interweaving of the estate of reality, of nature and God and ourselves!

5:26–28. The dark side of great fortunes: the great houses are built with mortar laced strongly with human blood.

The images are precise. Hunters lie in wait for unwary birds; so do the powerful lurk, on the alert for human victims. Then: the hunters "fill their cage full of birds, their houses full of loot." All those elegant furnishings, evidence beyond words of high culture, self-conscious and grandiose!

To the prophet, something else is at work, something malign beyond words. The possessions possess the owners, the "collectors"; wealth, power, great houses—these have other, darker meanings. They fill the eye and heart with the pride of life.

One imagines Jeremiah welcomed into such a house, ill at ease, evaluating with a cold eye the grandiosities, dismissing them with a single contemptuous word: "loot." To his cold eye the grandeur is no more than plunder, larceny on a grand scale. It was won at the price of the misery of "widows and orphans"—that cliché of the prophets, denoting the victims, a judgment hovering over the great ones of the world.

5:30–31. Jeremiah seems both fascinated and appalled.

A consonance has grown—like a night-blooming flower sown of greed and pride—between structures of evil. Worse and worse, the structures would name themselves "religious." It is a complicity admirable, efficient, simple. A dovetailing of self-interest; priest craft and pseudo-prophecy consummate a marriage of convenience. The stipulation: the prophets consult Baal; the priests announce, straight-faced, the oracles of the Dark One.

And the people? They "offer no objection," they "love it so."

Thus the apparatus works to everyone's satisfaction; for a time.

Everyone? But what of those "widows and orphans," the nameless ones, the outsiders? Let it be said straight: these simply do not count. Let Jeremiah remember them, plead for them if he so choose; those in the saddle of power ride on.

A form of "triage" is functionally useful. If the interests of the few are to be served, then many, a great multitude in truth, must be placed "outside the loop."

We too have seen it, and suffered under it. And shall see more of it, a mounting cruelty, socialized, hideously normalized.

The word is out; the votes are in. To wit: a few count for much, many count not at all. Let the latter eke out existence as best they might. If they lose heart, let them die. It is all the same to the powerful, the politicians and economists and bankers and tycoons.

All the same to religion?

Not, it would seem, all the same to Yahweh. He has a question, a terrible one. The passage ends, the question hovers on the air, unanswered. Unanswered, because unanswerable? The question: "What will they do when it all comes to an end?" Or (more directly): "What will you do... ?"

Which is to inquire, with guileful insight: Has the system, together with its architects and votaries, devised a "backup plan"?

The retort is laced with a kind of quizzical bad faith. But why should they require a second plan ("they" who are also "you") when the present scheme of things is working to their advantage?

Thus Jeremiah sees us: humans locked into the subhuman. Bolts and bars and a triple moat—captive to the culture of death. And who shall liberate us Lazarines, draw us forth to the land of the living, unbind us "from darkness and the shadow" (from the "filthy rotten system" assailed by Dorothy Day)?

They (we) had not thought of it, or taken it in account.

And for this reason, according to the prophetic critique; complicity with the system has killed the imagination, has foreclosed alternatives.

And we note that the imperial imagination, its images of absolute dominion, possesses the victims as well.

No, we had given no thought to "when it all comes to an end." The system simply does not admit to its lexicon that word, "the end." There is to be no—end.

The politics of power, the wolfish economy, the military muscle, the compliant religion—the "system," in sum, commends itself. It is in no need of carping critics. It is self-congratulatory, dwells with satisfaction on the evidence of greatness: its cornucopia of consumer goods, its arms research, its control of world markets. It owns the present, encompasses and claims the future. It is, in its own estimate, the final, ideal form of humanity.

In the eyes of fabricators and compliant beholders alike, the arrangement is so nearly perfect, it dazzles and stuns. (Even as it enslaves. But this was never said.) What could bring it down?

And then we hear that awful word, that counter, that trumpet blast: it is all to be brought down, and soon. (Is "sooner the better" implied?)

4
Ruin, Hope (6:1–30)

C hapter 6, all of it, is a vivid résumé of a polemic familiar to us, stark, febrile—and now nearing realization: no one, it appears, has attended to the word of Jeremiah; no hearts have turned round. Therefore ruin. The wheels of war are in motion; the catastrophe previously threatened is underway.

Yahweh's Threats: An Offer to Change the Heart (6:1–8)

6:3, 4. Jerusalem is hemmed in. Among the besiegers, various battle plans are bruited about. Day or night, what serves our advantage? Uncertainty riles the enemy camp. (Uncertainty also on our part, as to the point of the text!)

Is the vivid account a reminder to the besieged that the attack, when it comes, will be a matter of life and death? that the besieged had best take seriously, if not the admonitions of the prophet, then the guile and ferocity of the enemy?

6:7, 8. An image, robust, adroit: Jeremiah flings it like a stone straight at brow or heart: "As a well keeps its water fresh, so Jerusalem keeps its wickedness fresh." Nothing stale, nothing banal about evil; at least this evil! Wickedness is drawn from the well's depths, ever clear (clearly evil? yes, at least to the prophet).

And ever renewed, poured out, multiplied, serviceable, necessary it would seem, vessel on vessel drawn to the brim, without diminishment, by generation on generation...

Who tires of such waters? Who says "enough"? Each day we thirst again; we draw upon a dark source that seems literally boundless.

And another time warp. It is as though one viewed an old etching: the God of weathers, cheeks inflated, blows sturdily into a ship's sails. The canvas billows, the ship speeds on. Or another scene: this God wields thunders and lightnings, and since the time of Homer's intrepid sailors, humans run pell-mell for cover.

Here we have a change of note, an altering of transcendent weathers. The brow of Yahweh clears of its frowning. For the moment he relents of his threats of total destruction: "People of Jerusalem, let these troubles be a warning to you, or else I will abandon you" (v. 8).

And the enemy's prospects, formerly so strong as to seem invincible, also recede. Like the Jerusalemites, they too cannot succeed of their purpose, unless the hand of the Omnipotent One be raised in command.

Nothing is automatic here; much depends on mood, occasion, behavior of ourselves. We humans are not automatons; neither does God resemble the gods, those dei ex machina. The threats and fulminations, whatever their substance, import or outcome, are a tribute to the humanity of God and the tribe, alike.

God has godly ideas concerning us humans! We are free, which is to say—freely invited to distance ourselves from an enslaving culture, to summon and partake of our own humanity. Thus the threats of Yahweh pay tribute to our dignity. Launched with remarkable single-mindedness, they urge upon a tough, intransigent people, a change of heart.

Thus too an anthropology is hinted at. And a question is raised: What people, then or since, is to be thought other than tough and intransigent? A change of heart is demanded, of the Jerusalemites, of us.

A corporate examen of conscience is thus declared in order. Behavior is to be reviewed, failures noted: matters of justice, compassion, welcoming of the innocent and helpless, of widows and orphans. (So we question ourselves: How are issues of justice and compassion dealt with by church communities, in face of contrary winds of racism, sexism, homophobia?)

Suffering, Scorn,
Then Hope (6:9–11)

Another image, serendipitous indeed; and awful in implication: "Israel will be stripped clean like a vineyard from which every grape has been picked."

And an incendiary dialogue between Yahweh and Jeremiah is underway. One marvels that the page does not of itself ignite.

The public scene is demented, determined as people are on what amounts to self-destruction. And what is to be done? Are our two clairvoyants, Yahweh and the prophet, at one another's beck, discussing ways of salvaging this one or that, even a few? It would seem so: "You must rescue everyone while there is still time." There is still time, though the time shortens, like daylight when autumn draws the shades close.

And Jeremiah answers. He admits of no concession, no lackey he. He assumes responsibility, and is angry as well. The fury of Yahweh burns in him; he has swallowed fire.

His is a highly personal plaint, and painful beyond words. To paraphrase: "It is you who are at fault, and on more counts than one. You have commanded me to speak the truth, when (as you well know) the truth I speak lodges nowhere. Your word? It ricochets and falls away; ears are turned to stone."

A true "other," this Jeremiah, an opposite—even, when called for, an opposing force, a face of stone. A disciple yes, but frequently and daringly at odds. His own man, not to be absorbed or consumed or assimilated, even by the holiest of fires.

He knows it, he suffers under it. Sorrowfully, all that was foretold in his youth is coming true before his appalled eyes. That initial word concerning the morally blind, the deaf; and then the cost of speaking up, not only a willful ignoring, but fierce opposition: "All will be against you!" (1:18–19).

Yahweh knows the human heart, our predilection for untruth, self-deception, the sorry pleasures of delay and denial. And then comes the fury that kindles within, against the reprover, the man of intrepid judgment. Yahweh knows consequence: knows what lies ahead for the truth-teller, the truth-doer.

Jeremiah heard the dire prediction, years before. But a word, even an appalling word, is one thing—its coming true another.

And what of the present? Yes, it is shadowed. Still, as we commonly say, it is "not that bad." So something masquerading as hope, vain or spurious or mixed as it may be, beats on.

And somehow or other, with small measure of verve and joy, we keep keeping on. Pushing, as it were, that ominous gathering wave, away, ahead of us. But only wait. The wave gathers an appalling force. And true hope has yet to become itself, which is to say, to be reborn into "hope against hope."

At this stage of his life, even a Jeremiah has much to learn. Something like: everything bad is to get, so to speak, badder. He has yet to see event, evidence, experience, fidelity, plain truthfulness, his dire and so true analysis of his culture—all come to naught, turn against him, "evidence for the prosecution." Rejection and scorn and physical suffering lie ahead. A rocky path indeed!

And toward the end of that awful way, when nothing remains of self-justification, self-will, even the satisfaction of truth vindicated—then genuine hope may arise. Will arise.

He will see the ground give way beneath his feet, a chasm open: scorn, obloquy, spleen, and—perhaps worst of all—a dispiriting stupor meet his passionate, tormented face. Then his world, its atmosphere, the working of its institutions, will grow monstrously inhuman.

He is on an awful road, harsh, exhausting, seemingly going nowhere, a tremendous fictional path, a perennial deception and detour. And to all that: No! He is on the right road, traced by the finger of God, "writing straight with crooked lines." The right road for this pilgrim of the absolute, this "pilgrim of no progress."

One day he hears a distant thunder. It is the roar of the dragon in the way. He will take the monster on, and he will be—defeated. "[The beast] was allowed to do battle with the saints, and to overcome them" (Rev. 13:7).

This we shall see.

The Empire of Ananke: Soon to Be Dross (6:11–30)

6:11–15. Crime upon crime, threat following threat. The image is old as the once holy and great city, a city gone to moral ruin. Perfidy of every kind—greed and illicit gain ride high and mighty. And in this sordid frenzy, the prophets and priests play a large part; they pacify the people and normalize the abhorrent situation. "Not so bad, not so bad." "Peace, peace, and there is no peace."

6:16, 17. Yahweh moves to avert the impending catastrophe. The first act is an instruction to the people: "Seek out the ancient paths, and walk in them, and you will find rest for your souls." The occasion of the instruction, we are told, was the discovery of the book of Deuteronomy, hidden for long ages in the temple and only recently recovered (2 Kings 22:8ff.).

We may judge the depth of the loss from the consequence—the loss, not of a book, but of an entire tradition. For centuries the law of Yahweh had been put to silence, the community deprived of its primal resource.

How compile a structure of morality? The task lay beyond the powers of priests or kings or counselors. A debacle was inevitable. The era of the prophets arrived; idolatry and injustice tainted the society: "Kings, officials of Judah, priests and people..." (it could as well be added, certain among the prophets themselves, those who played sedulous acolytes to princes).

The litany of loss summons to mind a people lost in inanition of spirit, blindly falling away. Their malaise is summed up and dramatized in the mockery that greets the word of God, as announced by Jeremiah.

We note a crowning irony. Even as the long lost book of the law is opened once more, the word of God meets only with rejection.

Yet the book had counseled again and again, as though moral amnesia were the worst of imaginable illnesses: "Make certain that you do not forget your God. Do not fail to observe any of the laws I am giving you today" (Lev. 8:11 and passim).

The people forget, massively, for generations. There follow idolatry and its grim-faced twin, injustice, the behavioral consequence of false worship. We have dolorous images here, of a society utterly at odds with itself and the world at large—a soulless *massa damnata*.

In the circumstance, the discovery of the lost scroll and the determined reform of King Josiah are crucial. The people must know this. Jeremiah is issued his orders: "Stand at the crossroads." They are indeed at a crossroads, a choice must be made, and quickly. "Ask for the ancient path, where the good road is."

Ask whom? The answer is left to them—and to us as well. To us who know well Whom to ask. And so often renege on asking. Who prefer to construct and dwell in a slapped-up, rickety shack, a morality of our own devising. A morality that, in sum, justifies and vindicates our appetite for power and dominion.

We presumed for a long time that we knew the good road, the right one. The only one. But it was deceitfully posted, a dead-end. It went nowhere. It led to a bastardized, Americanized religion. We were, truth told, Christian Americans. The point was the noun: Americans. The ever-so-slight modifier, the adjective: Christian. Christians took on the coloration of America, its ethos of violence and greed and racism and the rest. For all practical purposes, we all but disappeared, assimilated, in the empire.

Certain aspects of our own story are hinted at in the books of Maccabees. The story is profoundly disturbing. Some among the Jews allowed, approved, finally aided the fierce incursion of paganism known as the "hellenization" of the holy city. (The abstraction, as usual, conceals extraordinary moral ugliness.)

For good reason the Greeks had elevated the principle of "necessity" to the status of a goddess, Ananke. Under her tutelage, hellenization becomes—inevitable. Willy-nilly, the Jews are to be drawn into the Empire of Necessity. Ancient she is; as old as Old Egypt, that place well set in Jewish memory, an abode of exiles and slaves—themselves.

"Narrow," "throat"—the verbs "strangle" and "constrict" apply. Dame Ananke takes you by the throat, leads you by the strait and narrow, into slavery. "The gods have become diseases" (Jung).

This was hardly to be thought a process, more or less sensible, of imposing a few cultural nonessentials on a people. The truth was brutal: a "final solution." A decree of extermination was in force; Jews were to abandon the faith or disappear from the earth. And a certain number went over to the Kingdom of Necessity. They turned quislings, betrayed the faith, abandoned their sisters and brothers.

Jeremiah's sense is that a kind of internal apostasy is brewing. The people have already given over what the tyrant at the gates would take from them. Ananke rules. And Jeremiah would open the true way. He walks it, knows it.

Are we to take counsel from him—that beginning anew, starting over, is a form of wisdom? (A sorry form at best, but a true one.)

Of capital note: when an inquiry is raised as to the right way, the presumption is clear—the finger points, the way is close at hand. It is simple as that; for this reason the prophet exists in their midst. They have only to seek the way and it will be pointed out. What remains is to "walk the walk," in the "good way." But the people were adamant: "We will not walk in it."

Yahweh breathes deep; he will try again: "I set watchman over you, saying: Listen for the sound of the trumpet" (v. 17). Trumpet of war, trumpet of approaching doom, trumpet of judgment imminent? A warning, in any case; heeded, it will avert or at least mitigate the threatened ruin.

The "watchmen" are the prophets of that extraordinary century. Who could adequately praise this magnificent roster, the glory of our race, mystics in action, these courageous, oneiric geniuses? They form a choral ode of truth, every note a glory: Jeremiah, Zephaniah, Habakkuk, Nahum, Ezekiel. These hearken and obey.

But the people said: "We will not listen."

6:20. An old theme is raised, and a constant one among those alert "watchmen": Of what value before Yahweh are symbols stripped of all substance? "Incense,... spices,... burnt offerings,... sacrifices..." The litany bespeaks moral emptiness, offerings rendered mephitic by the day-to-day behavior of the congregation—odious, meretricious, predatory, devoid of compassion as they are.

6:27–30. It is suggested that we are here offered a summary of the first part of Jeremiah's ministry (chaps. 1–6), and yet another image of the seer: he is a metallurgist. He purges in a furnace the substance of his people, separating silver from dross.

And all in vain, it appears: "The wicked are not separated."

5
The Temple, an Idol? Yes!
(7:1–8:22)

Sacrifice, Public Behavior, All One (7:1–16)

7:1–3. Eventually it becomes clear that the king's reforms have failed. Too little, too late. And the prophet, who digs to the root of things, diagnoses with a kind of merciless mercy, and goes unheard. Jeremiah has no stomach for "reform."

The people, in any case, are unimpressed with the king's earnest homilies. The "old ways" of Deuteronomy, austere and minatory, win few hearts or minds.

Then, perturbation on high. Jeremiah is told to go preach at the gate of the temple—a task that might be thought bootless in the extreme.

Only consider: this is the magnificent temple of Solomon. A recent event has underscored once more the numinous character of the place—a discovery in the temple precincts; a sacred object, a kind of Dead Sea Scroll. The event was taken by authorities as a watershed in the religious life of the populace. The lost text of the law lay in their hands! There was much talk of new beginnings, even of a new covenant with Yahweh.

Talk and more talk. Alas, something far different from spiritual renewal hung heavy on the air: idolatry toward the temple itself. Jeremiah sensed it: "The temple of the Lord, the temple of the Lord, the temple of the Lord!" He mocked without mercy the incantation, the resorting to magic. In substance, he implied, the babble differed not a whit from a ululation raised in favor of this or that idol.

Meantime the authorities, out of touch, shortly overreached themselves. Noses on high, they assumed that the newfound book of the law would be taken seriously; efforts were undertaken toward a thoroughgoing reform. The excellent intentions proved fruitless. Little or nothing changed; the social misbehavior that so exercised Jeremiah proceeded as before.

"The temple of the Lord!" The formula, purportedly expressing veneration of a holy place, acted only as a cover. Illusion reigned; surely nothing ill can befall while the temple stands, serene, sumptuous, our glory.

As to events impending, a belief lay implicit in the liturgical mimicry. The implication was this: there will be no invasion. Unthinkable! And further: we need change nothing of our behavior. God is at our behest, no matter the eructations of this surly one, Jeremiah.

"The church that is not reborn through suffering, but merely rearranged in its domestic life, only succeeds in becoming more efficiently fascist" (Paulo Freire). Indeed and alas, yes.

Jeremiah is told: Go then, stand in that place that they declare mine, when in truth it is theirs alone—their nest of illusion, of idolatry. Speak the truth in the place of untruth.

Are they immune in those precincts? Are they safe throughout the land—merely because the Ark of the Covenant is intact? Utter a great no!—unwelcome, unpalatable as the word is bound to be.

7:5–10. We are not to conclude that Jeremiah is here (or elsewhere) offering a list of defaults—one among them being worship of false gods. No. Each catalog of crimes ends, in fact, with the name of the greatest of crimes: idolatry.

He digs deep; in truth, idolatry permeates every misdeed. They are unjust toward one another, taking base advantage of widows and orphans, even killing the innocent (v. 6). Such behavior already implies (as insisted on in the same verse) "worshiping false gods."

And so with verse 9: "You put trust in deceitful words, steal, murder, commit adultery, tell lies under oath." And immediately: "You offer sacrifices to Baal, worship gods you have not known before." According to the diatribe, violations of the Decalogue lead to, even as they proceed from, false worship.

The character of Baal? He is a god to whom all things are morally equal. What a convenient deity! No judgment, no accountability—no evil in fact, and no goodness. The categories are irrelevant.

Thus the god stands, along with Astarte, the "queen of heaven" (v. 18), for a world of nature that has been tamed and brought to heel. The seasons are obedient and fruitful in their cycle. No transcendence is implied, no moral consequence. Only give us such gods!

7:11. Yahweh's temple, "My temple": Is it to become a place of refuge for thieves? a "den of thieves"? (Matt. 21:13). Jesus, we note, objected forcefully to the huckstering of wares in the precincts.

Here the emphasis is different. Once the presence of Yahweh is ignored, Jeremiah implies, prayer, biblical truth-telling, occasions for repentance, all vanish. The temple is transformed; it is now the refuge of a criminal people.

Then, now, what make of such places?

A story comes to mind. In the National (*sic*) Cathedral in Washington, D.C., a service was held on August 5, 1995. A large congregation from near and far assembled to commemorate the fiftieth anniversary of the atomic destruction of Hiroshima.

A week before the event, we who were invited to speak received a text by mail. We were abruptly informed that words of our own choosing, or overt reference to the great crime of atomic bombing, were disallowed. My text seemed eminently safe, wide of the mark: a selection from a medieval mystic. In the course of the evening, an authority of the cathedral arose, introducing himself as the "ethicist in residence." He recalled the glories of the place: Dr. Martin Luther King had delivered his last sermon there; Archbishop Tutu had preached. Then he added words to this effect: that "the cathedral took no position on the morality of nuclear weapons, or indeed of any other political [*sic*] question."

Martin Sheen, also invited to speak, looked at me in blank disbelief. I arose to my cue, venturing to thank the official for recalling the great spirits who had graced the temple. But I added that I found it difficult to imagine Dr. King ascending the pulpit to declare his peace with a "position of no position, on racism."

I intended to speak in a like vein of Desmond Tutu, and a "no position" on apartheid. But I was interrupted by deafening applause as the congregation rose to its feet, after the first sentence was uttered.

As result of this modest effort at truth-telling, on the following morning several hundred congregants fared forth to the Pentagon demonstration. I suspect that prior to the modest encounter of the previous evening, many among them had not intended to do so.

7:12. A bit of history is of help here in decoding the text. Shiloh, the amphictyonic center of tribes, was destroyed during the Philistine Wars. The catastrophe would be remembered in nearby Anathoth, the hometown of Jeremiah. Allusion (he alone makes it) to the catastrophe is even more plausible if Jeremiah is a descendant of the priests who dwelt in Anathoth during the time of exile.

Take it to heart, you people. This is the daring midrash of Jeremiah: the fate of Shiloh can become the fate of "My temple."

But is the vast pile in reality to be thought "Mine"?

"You do those things I hate, and then you come and stand in My presence, in My own temple, and say: 'We are safe.'" Only think: what goes forth, returns. Sacrifice, public behavior, it is all one. The theme will be drummed, century after century, prophet after prophet. As though from hill to hill, heartbeat, soul, were being passed on. The crimes here denounced, renounced, are in reality "never done with." Our crimes, a dark legacy. The sin named original, ever and darkly made new.

As to the temple then, rather than "Mine," awfully—it is "yours," your legacy, your moral void manifest in stone.

"What I did at Shiloh I will do to this temple of Mine, in which you trust." Shocking, on the face of it: the God of the temple threatens the destruction of the temple. And did it not occur?

7:16. "Do not plead.... Do not cry.... Pray... for this people, for I will not listen to you." What a dire command! Sublime, tragic, heartfelt. An instruction to be sure—and all the while implying its opposite.

Which is to say: turn the command around, act in contrariety; cry, pray, plead, persuade, intercede. Rage. We have here (and elsewhere to be sure) an irony of note. Behind the words that seem so adamant, a heartbeat is heard—and heard in the very words. It beats on, pleads, cries out—the heart of Yahweh.

God's anger must be "deconstructed" (as the clumsy word goes). This anger veils a longing for Jeremiah's plea and intercession. Otherwise, one asks, of what point the words? Is not a plea implied in the command to cease and desist?

In effect: Do not give up on this people! Even as I in addressing you, and you taking heed—as we together, in concert of hope and compassion, refuse to give up on them.

The Socializing of Sin (7:17–31)

The practical workings of idolatry are set down with exactness, recalling to mind a parallel passage in Isaiah (44:9–20). Yahweh, one assumes, is keeping a close eye on "these people"—who for the moment are not to be named "My people." And this is the spectacle that meets his gaze: everyone is industrious, earnest, involved in a mischievous bustling about—the preparations for (so-called) worship. And by now the affront is generational.

The children are enlisted, "gathering firewood." And the men, "making fires." And the women, "mixing dough to make cakes for the goddesses...." And, one infers, the priests, hovering in the wings.

Everyone goes about the appointed tasks in a tranquil, apparently responsible, spirit. It is as though sleepwalkers were abroad, or a madhouse were being mimed. There is no discussion; no one objects or intervenes. And each can take modest credit for a part in tasks that on the face of it make perfect sense: fueling the stove, building fires, baking.

We have the socializing of sin, its mimetic power, the passage of quite normal, quotidian activities into perilous areas: the normalizing of the abnormal. In no real sense has the scroll of Deuteronomy been recovered. To the contrary: the formerly abhorrent has become the norm.

A new moral measure of work, of mutuality, of the meaning of worship, of the human itself is before us.

7:21–28. Jeremiah is well aware that "burnt sacrifices" and "whole sacrifices" are part of the original covenant, that the ordinances surrounding these liturgies are older than the exile (Leviticus 1–7). Yet he calls each of them—useless; "you might as well eat them all."

More: in 7:21, he denies flatly that Yahweh included such forms as part of the code of covenant (though the opposite is clear from Exod. 20–23 and Deut. 12:1ff.). Here is Jeremiah, quoting Yahweh: "I gave no orders about burnt offerings or any kinds of sacrifices, on the day I brought your ancestors out of Egypt." (The citation of "the day" is crucial—on that day that surpassed all days, a day when the liberating acts of God reached their ultimate point of providential love.) He contradicts—blatantly, assuredly—Exodus and Deuteronomy. How explain the contradiction, astonishing on the face of it?

We have a clue in yet another passionate outburst of Jeremiah. More: the soul of the ethic of prophecy itself. This or that sacrifice, this or that ritual, this or that—yes, temple—of what matter to Me? Of no matter! The heart, the heart—give it over to God! Away with your sacrifices and semblances and blank overtures and hypocrisies and meaningless chatter, one and all masking a ferocious appetite for evil!

At 7:23 Yahweh (a great one for memory) forces a recollection: "I did command them to obey Me,...so that things would go well for them." And not just "told you." The text proceeds; it is clear that God remembers well, and in detail, the works and words of God. As to an amnesiac people, unmindful and uncaring of their own story—quite literally they require a re-minding. And here receive it.

Of import is not only right instruction, but the integrity and fidelity of the one who utters it, the quality of the one who speaks the truth, having first embodied it. Jeremiah.

Back to beginnings: it is as though Yahweh is dealing with children. "From the day your ancestors came out of Egypt"—and so on. Yahweh sent a line of prophets, generations long, one after another. A delicious note: "Daily rising early, I sent them" (NASB).

Despise them as you will, dispose of them in favor of corrupt law and order. And so send a signal of contempt for Yahweh. Nonetheless, they remain your sole glory, valiant, prodigiously eloquent, towering in moral stature, ardent and harsh in love, clairvoyant, fiery. And now another prophet encounters the same "hard hearts" (the word is properly Jeremiah's, and often repeated). They turn away.

Jeremiah is directly addressed by Yahweh, high credentials are conferred; he is placed squarely in the line of great clairvoyants. His credentials are of God, and his words are lost on vagrant winds of indifference.

7:29–30. Of false cults and punishment to follow. Life has taken a cruel turn; lamentation is the only adequate response. This is true of victim-survivors; they know how to mourn. But to a criminal people, mourning seems ethically and psychologically repugnant.

An opposite response: the emotional life goes mad, even as the moral life is rent asunder. So it follows: crimes that cry to heaven for redress (even as Jeremiah's Yahweh cries out)—such abominations are transformed. The moral order is toppled; perversity and malice triumph. Socialized crime becomes an immense wellspring of national glory, the exalted subject of poetry, sculpture, parades, Te Deums.

Then and now.

7:31. Far astray are these, the architects of their own morality, who have no need of God's law. Far from the God they choose to despise.

God speaks in a kind of befuddled wonderment: "And it did not come into My mind..." (i.e., that they sacrifice their own children).

We of the failing twentieth century declare in horror: "How far we stand from such abominations!" And yet how near in actuality—the actuality of war, of urban violence, of inferior schools, of bad housing, of no medical care, of no future.

The children of the affluent are sacrificed as well, in the fires of greed and consumerism. And children are sacrificed massively to gods of war, repeatedly, relentlessly: the Iraqis, the Panamanians, the Guatemalans, the Vietnamese—"burning their sons and daughters in the fire."

On the part of the God of life, a stupefied horror. Could such perpetrators of infamy be considered the summit and crown of creation? Could the tribe called human conceive such crimes, then contrive the weaponry to carry them out?

"I did not command them to do such things, nor did it even enter my mind."

A Tribe of Corpses (7:32–8:3)

7:34. All rejoicing, all occasions of celebration, are removed. A brief threnody is interjected here, as a massive scene of death, both socialized and spiritual, unfolds.

A kind of geographical history emerges. The scene of the initial crimes, the murder of children, is hardly unattended or ignored. It becomes the symbolic scene of nature's (or Yahweh's) revenge. Adults have sacrificed children to their gods. Very well then, let the adults also perish; and at the scene of their abomination.

8:1. So in that place an outcome, altogether befitting: the corpses of idolaters are exhumed and lie unburied. It is as though the eye of God surveys the charnel field. The identity of the dishonored dead, their function in life, their betrayal of the code of life are devastatingly, unlovingly dwelt upon.

The disinterred include all classes: "the bones of the kings of Judah and the bones of the princes and the bones of the priests and the bones of the prophets and the bones of the inhabitants of Jerusalem." They lie there exposed "to the sun, the moon, and to all the host of heaven, which they have loved and which they have served and which they have gone after and which they have sought and which they have worshiped."

In a terrible final curse, the bones are scattered, given over to the gods they worshiped in life, "as dung on the face of the ground." (The rhetoric of Jeremiah's sermon is devastating. It calls to mind the thunderous cadences of Martin Luther King; the words are best read aloud.)

8:3. Yahweh reports directly on the fate of the demoralized survivors. What of them? They fare no better than the dead, turning as they do a blind eye to crime and consequence.

Shall they be called "the living"? They are no more alive, to God, to one another, than stalking corpses. Driven far and wide, a tribe of Cain, their behavior turns the earth they tread to a mortuary. They walk in the old ways, "the sensual sty of utility" (Croce). They choose death; their behavior mimes that of the dead.

Such is Jeremiah's blinding insight into the fate of the morally blind—how sin is passed on, a cursed legacy, normalized, generational. Nothing is learned, nothing changes.

Jeremiah invites pondering into the later understanding of "state of sin," of "original sin."

Foolishness Crowns Your Days (8:4–22)

8:4–7 The people turn, turn about—
heads askew
hearts at odds,
no repenting!

Why, see the storks
soaring high heaven
near, afar, unerring
as arrows, to nest—
turtledove, thrush,
swift birds of passage
heedful of seasons
seemly, timely
migrating, returning—

Only this people
ignorant, termagant
driven, unknowing

uncaring of Me, My
dear heart's covenant
enfolding and freeing!

8:8–12 How then declare, "We are wise"
when foolishness crowns your days?

And "God's word dwells in us"—
lo, worldly traffic buzzing?

Priest, prophet, scribe—
anarchic, deceitful, every one.
False healing, meager faith;
a cry: "Peace, peace!" at lip,
and the warrior heart aflame—
sword unsheathed, at the ready.

Day of discord, day of doom.
My wrath
unsheathed, at the ready!

8:18–22 Jeremiah:
sorrow beyond healing,
heart faint within me.
Hear it, an exile's cry;
abandoned I am, my God
far, far as clouds that brood
anarchic, unmoored
in a blameless sky!

Ringaround, season and season
in sweet ordaining;
planting, scything, sheathing,
harvests abundant.

Our portion—famine.
Nettles, grubs, wasting hungers.
Is there in Gilead
no balm?
What of our wounds, where
in the world, that
wounded Healer?

6
Your Deeds Stink of Wormwood (9:1–10:25)

Jeremiah Weeps: For Good Reason (9:1–16)

9:1–6 Tears, tears be my meed,
        tears in a desert waste—
        the slain, the innocent
        laid low, and no recourse!

        They prevail, the great ones,
        deceitful, deadly,
        a plague of arrows.

        Each against each, rumor
        thick sown as tares—
        crafty, vigilant,
        doors iron-barred.

        What care you, uncaring
        of me—you scorners
        of love, of law?

9:1–3. The tears of Jeremiah, that great heart of his quite overwhelmed! And what wonder? Who has not longed as he does, to flee a disastrous scene? He weeps for no slight cause. And no one attends his tears; no one hears him out.

His defeat has been laid down by Yahweh, a very law of iniquity at work. He is to be rejected by his peers, even by family (11:19; 12:6) and friends (20:10).

9:3–6. And he knows why. His social analysis is devastating. In the war of myths, Yahweh vs. the Baals, Baal has prevailed; truth is the first casualty.

So the mourning prophet speaks of sins of the tongue, the "bending of a bow" awry, the "arrow" of speech wobbling along unsteadily, far from its target, the truth. In such an atmosphere each stands guard against his neighbor; trust has vanished from the earth.

9:9. And again a summons of Yahweh is issued: to judgment, to vengeance even. Yet be it noted, the summons is put in the form of a question: "Shall I not take vengeance on such a people?" It is as though once more God were inviting the prophet to protest against a harsh decree, to plead for the wrongdoers.

9:10. Which he proceeds to do. And indirectly, with great delicacy. His role vis-à-vis the people is in no wise altered. Heart to heart with Yahweh he stands, God's surrogate on earth. Yet this favored one pleads time and again for the recalcitrants, inviting God to reconsider both crime and punishment.

Must not Yahweh too, he implies, love greatly his creation, degraded and befouled though it be by an unconscionable people? The holy ones must mourn together; Jeremiah initiates the threnody: "For the mountains,…weeping and wailing, for the pastures,…a dirge."

No greater lover of the creation than Jeremiah, no more bitter mourner for its despoiling. The theme is obsessive and recurring. All is in ruins. Where once the creation flourished, a wasteland stretches to the horizon: no humans, no cattle; birds and beasts vanished from the earth. Beings that flew and raced free and sang and bellowed, barked and screeched and roared; all that lends joy to eye and ear and touch and taste, that awes and inspires and renders the seeing heart grateful—entire species have been made to disappear.

The oracle is of today, of ourselves.

9:12–16. The poetic dirge is interrupted by a prose passage (vv. 12–16), a midrash that questions and answers as well (better still, rebuts) the earlier poem of Jeremiah. Someone has read the text with care, and with a kind of footnote dared correct it.

And the unknown objector is not happy! a scribe perhaps, an apologist for the reform initiated after the discovery of the Deuteronomy scroll. (There is yet another theory concerning the unique poetry-prose form, the "sequence of rebuttal." According to this hypothesis, the prose was composed as a commentary to go along with the liturgical reading of the original dirge. But does this dispose of the strong sense that a "rebuttal" is underway?)

Someone, in short, "deconstructed" the thunderous anger, the dark mood that predicted (and appointed) the dead-end of humanity's quest. Someone, at most some few, hearkened, obeyed, believed; they preserved, assembled, set down the entire scroll.

Against all odds, prophecy reaches far and farther: first to a few among Jeremiah's compatriots; later, as far as ourselves, the generations to come. Gratefully, we know the word did not die, despite the awful predictions of Yahweh to the contrary.

Some few, a believing remnant, passed on the great word. Including this word, for warning—that the word of Yahweh would go largely unheeded. Thus thanks to the likes of Jeremiah, we have Yahweh surpassing Yahweh, in the holy combat of hope against hope.

The teaching method of the prophet takes a Socratic form. Themes are relentlessly pursued and questioned, under a score of different images. "Why is the land...laid waste?" The wise one knows, we are assured, knows the right questions, reads the signs aright. And Yahweh responds; and we listen and grow wise. Or at least grow less awfully foolish. "Because they have forsaken My law..."

We have heard it before; it is as old as the book of Genesis and the Fall. Good or ill, the community may read aright its moral estate in the mirror of natural creation. Things flourish, things fall apart; but the outcome is by no means haphazard, by chance or mischance or a cast of the dice.

We have seized the apple of discord. More terribly by far, we have murdered our brother. We are the first parents; we are the fratricide Cain. Every generation comes on its perverse way of originating, once more, the forms of sin. Every generation has "forsaken My law," has "not obeyed My voice," has "walked after the Baals."

An ominous phrase follows the last image of malfeasance: "...as their fathers taught them." Jeremiah's Yahweh is a great one for uttering a shattering insight, thrust at us as though in passing, a kind of afterthought. Idolatry is passed on, parent to child, and on and on. So the original sin is never done with, repented, exorcised.

No new start. Sin is drawn out of history like a sword long resting in its scabbard. It is tested anew, whizzing and whining in the air. Practice makes perfect: the sword becomes newly "relevant," becomes attractive, becomes necessary, expedient—just. In every generation sin takes on a new, specious, vulpine originality. It is yours and mine, ours; it belongs to the living. It is our culture, a pantheon of Baals.

Here, as elsewhere, is suggested the gradual (or not so gradual) normalizing of the inherently abnormal. Father to son and so on. The fathers oversee the worship, the mothers prepare ovens for the bread of offering, the children gather wood. Everyone is involved, everything is normal. The Baals become a constant, a presence. They are matter of the air we breathe—the air polluted in the political jungle "out there," in the itching consumerism, in religion mute as to large issues and cumbering as to small.

And above all and permeating all, we note with horror (or we do not) the normalizing of violence, near and far, as a matter of daily record. A matter inevitably claiming us, our souls in servitude to a cannibal, spoliating beast.

In this cultural welter, where might the God of Jeremiah be found? Pushed to the sidelines, in the world he made.

Of uncommon moment in this regard is the implication of the dire words of Yahweh to the prophet (7:27): "You will speak these words to My people, but they will not listen; you will call but they will not answer." An old story: the same harsh word of spiritual foreclosure was conveyed to Isaiah. He also must face the stony of heart, the willfully blind (6:9–11).

At stake is the fate of the prophet. And more: his is equivalently the fate of Yahweh. If the word of God in the estimate of humans is beside the point of human life, then so is the God who utters the word. In declaring that God's prophet will be denied a hearing in the recusant world, God is declaring the fate of God in the same world. This is plain to see, a pattern, Jeremiah to Jesus, history and hallucination, both.

The rejection of the word declares, as well, the fate of the human tribe. In two terrifying images: "I will feed them, this people [no longer, we note, 'My people'], with wormwood, and give them poisoned water to drink" (9:15). And then: "I will scatter them among the nations . . . and send the sword after them until I have annihilated them" (9:16).

Ecological consequence shadows the irresponsible ones. Food and drink are gone to poison; the earth cannot sustain the clan, guileful, appalling, unconscionable. The ecology is degraded, sign and consequence of the degradation of our sorry selves.

And a second sign: the "scattering among the nations."

Your Deeds Stink of Wormwood (9:1–10:25)

Is not this the sense of the threat—that the "scattering" has already occurred, that the words announce a fait accompli? Everything of substance has been squandered, then abandoned; everything good is a former good, a matter of a holy history long since renounced.

Once for all the book is closed. That scroll, unheeded, unread as it is, would, if attended to, tell a tale both inspiring and doleful: how a once faithful people observed covenant with fervor and devotion, worshiped a Yahweh known and reverenced. No longer. The people are internally colonized. The ways and means of "the nations" have infiltrated them, bone and marrow.

Ever so gently, guilefully, the community of faith is won over to other gods, other ways in the world. Was it for the sake of protective coloration? Was it cowardice, fear of sacrifice? Was it the lure of "silver, chariots, idols?" (Isaiah 2).

Does nothing of value survive? A certain rhetoric perhaps, gestures denoting obeisance, inert rites, and above all—properties, material claims and special interests and emoluments, also public honors duly paid; in sum, the residue of a faith gone dead, long buried. An impartial visitor would be hard put to note significant differences of behavior or attitude that might set this people apart. No conflicts with the larger culture, no moral objection or counter to the drift of resemblance to "the nations."

And then the third threat: "the sword." The word of God as a sword. The "annihilating" word—a weapon. This is the history, a nagging sorrow to Yahweh; again and again he returns to it, a lover obsessed with loss. "This people" have taken up the sword, and they have "forsaken My law."

The lost scroll, what a symbol! It was first of all lost to public esteem and obedience. Close the book! (That done, the word has lost its power over us. We are free to initiate war, to justify murder, to crush the widow and orphan.)

And for ourselves, we are given a word greater than Jeremiah's, a more stringent scroll than Deuteronomy. We have the word of Jesus as to matters of "love" and "enemies." And more: an irrefutable example, the life and death of this God in our midst.

Alas, time passes, and this scroll too is closed, is lost to view. There comes to us a beckoning from "the nations": May not our status in the world be improved? May not the scent, sweet and heady, of imperial approval be ours?

Then, something else, something awful. The scent is of death, of wormwood and poison. In effect the clan has come on a better way than the way of Jesus; shortly the people are "scattered among the nations." And quickly the teaching of the suffering savior, the one who chose to surrender his life rather than take life, is lost.

A lamentable reversal of role; better, of soul.

That people of covenant, ourselves, whose noble ancestry died by the sword—behold them now take the "annihilating sword" in hand! As Yahweh was dismissed, and the word was deemed irrelevant, so with the word of Jesus. How shall the two coexist, sword and word?

Say it plain, say it with your life: they cannot. The first victim was the word. The sword has annihilated the word.

Enter Death (9:17–26)

9:17–20. Summon the women who mourn. A custom of the time, we are informed; on occasion of calamity, professionals are called in. Could the women be taken as personifying the spirit of Jeremiah himself, his tears become the tears of all, his mourning the communal theme as catastrophe neared? So near indeed that like a storm presaging a greater storm, its tide all but overwhelms—even in prospect.

The women mourn and mourn. And we summon Jeremiah, mourning. His book is one vast dirge, a tide, a sea of tears for the genetic fault and folly of us humans. The women stand surrogate for all: for Jeremiah, so often in tears; for the slain youths and children; for the exiles; for the land, groaning under the jackboots of invaders; for the harvests lost through drought and pestilence.

9:21, 22. Then death enters the dwellings, personified, pestilential. The like image is borrowed by Hosea (13:14), by Isaiah (28:15–18), by Habakkuk (2:5), by the Psalmist (49:15), by Job (28:22).

The palace windows had opened on an emollient, lissome horizon of field and mountain, of sunstarts on coastal waters, on perspectives of faultless grandeur, season following season like a procession of gift-bearers. The holy city, the land so blessed!

Vanished now is all that beauty; vanished too the eyes that rejoiced to behold it. The same casements now grant to Death a sure entrance.

The carnage proceeds; it is the day of Death the Reaper. His scythe whispers, a wide swath, human sheaf upon sheaf. The innocent fall first; death has "cut down the children in the streets and the young men in the marketplaces."

We too have seen it, from Vietnam to Iraq to Northern Ireland to Israel-Palestine. The gods of war, grim reapers on rampage, shame upon shame. But how strange: the response is often contrary to nature; the mourners are few—and the revelers legion.

Thereby, a sure sign: we have lost the God who mourns—mourns for us, the lost.

9:23, 24. Put aside vain boasting, cast from heart and mind the debris of the world; power signifies nothing before Yahweh, nor does wealth!

Here Jeremiah touches on the apogee of the religion of Israel: true "knowledge" of God. God is self-revealed to the people of the code as the one of *hesed, mispat, sedaqa*—God of loving-kindness, righteousness, and justice.

In these three graces the self-revelation of Yahweh is complete—and the people are granted their full humanity. Or let us be more modest: the community is granted knowledge of the good, and is urged to follow it, and in quite sound and specific ways.

Need it be added that today we are hardly deprived of icons of the human? And in the great Trinity of Goodness poured out on us, we at once intuit and assuage and vitalize the deepest longing of our hearts: to act humanly in an inhuman world. What greater gift?

(The attributes of Yahweh here conferred were much in the mind of Hosea also [4:1–5; 5:4; 6:4; 8:2]. And Paul takes note of this sapiential passage, and quotes it with approval [1 Cor. 1:31; 2 Cor. 10:17].)

9:25, 26. Alas for the hope of God the Compassionate, Just, Righteous. Alas for ourselves, despising, canceling, sullying the gifts.

It comes to the same end, all said: the circumcised and the uncircumcised are undifferentiated. The Israelites are morally assimilated; they ape the "dwellers upon the earth." Ill-behavior contradicts the gift, cancels it out. And resemblance to the Holy One vanishes from the earth. There exists no "knowledge of Yahweh" to be rejoiced in. Rather, moral emptiness—where once flourished a people of moral alertness, determined on creating just structures, caring for the "widows and orphans."

A yawn, then an incantation: "Temple of Yahweh, temple of Yahweh"; empty liturgies, a rite signifying, truth told, the acceptability of a wicked secular "paraliturgy of behavior"—greed and violence. Hearts are uncircumcised: "The land is filled with chariots and silver and idols" (Isaiah 2).

Like calls unto like; the nations, in a spasm of cynical recognition, know the chosen for their own. Which is to say—Yahweh knows them not.

And what of the uncircumcised? They are cataloged here, but their crimes are hardly dwelt upon. Enough has been implied concerning them, in the castigations heaped on those they have won over to their dark ethos.

The Idols Belittled (10:1–25)

10:1–16. A "preventive" satire on idolatry, probably exilian, post-Jeremian. The implication is that the "chosen" are dwelling among pagans. (Of interest also is the gloss of v. 11, in Aramaic, possibly a liturgical interjection.)

The theme has been explored by Second Isaiah in much the same heavily ironic style (40:19–22; 44:9–20), and by the Psalmist (115:9–16; 135:15–18). The mockery is hilarious; the idols are toppled by a kind of prophet-clown. The images must be fastened with nails, or they totter uneasily. And they must be carried about; they cannot walk. They are "like a scarecrow in a field of cucumbers."

Yahweh assures: "They can do you no harm, neither can they do you any good."

No harm? What assurance! Yahweh speaks from an ample sense of who he is—and who the idols are not. Thus their "harm" is denied by one who stands at distance from their dark pretensions and power.

But as for ourselves, harm aplenty. Whence? We have seen it in our lifetime: those who yield up to death-dealing projects, scientific and otherwise, but always deadly—in a Faustian bargain they yield up their souls. The servitors are trapped; the idols own them.

Perhaps most pernicious of all, one's center eye is transfixed; attentiveness becomes a form of devotion—to that which has no existence, "the work of their hands." Distraction from the true way.

Simply put: sin. Giving over one's life to works of death, to artifacts that signify love of death, pursuit of death, the "way of death" in the world. Weapons, idols.

And the first to die are the makers and worshipers of idols. The idols are shortly to be destroyed also. Their demise is announced bluntly in verse 11. It is a matter of liturgical sanity, a reminder in the midst of worship—of the false worship in vogue: "Thus you shall say to them: 'The gods that did not make the heavens and the earth shall perish from the earth and from under the heavens.'"

A reminder:

If scientists heeded this call, to abandon the out of date thinking of the cold war, and instead, worked to abolish war altogether, then there would be no new nuclear warheads,... no new chemical and biological poisons. The arms race would be over.

Even if nuclear stockpiles are destroyed, the technology and risk of a new arms race will remain. The only way to prevent this is to abolish war altogether. The quest for a war-free world has a basic purpose: survival.

(Joseph Rotblat, Nobel Peace Prize Speech, 1995)

It is perhaps worth noting once more: abstract atheists do not inhabit the Bible; practical atheists do. And to all appearances, these latter much resemble a certain kind of believers. These are, in fact, also idolaters. Their behavior, a pretended mastery over life and death, gives them away. Today as in the time of Jeremiah, they operate under a cover of respectability. They are paragons of law and guardians of public order; it is the likes of Jeremiah, they intone, who are "the problem."

They regard themselves as models of the human, public benefactors. These are, for example, those judges who are livid with spleen and indignation when a nonviolent resister is brought before their court. Or they are nuclear-weapons researchers. No qualms disturb; they act, as they declare, in good conscience. Their work is in benefit of "national security," or it has "beneficial side-effects."

Such equivocation receives no approval from the likes of Jeremiah. As to his Yahweh: no approval; quite the opposite. What pleases this God of simplicity and grandeur is a confession: the God we worship is one, and has created all things. And all things are good. Adoration and confession of this befit the human, ennoble us.

The two contrarieties, true God and the idols, are here described. Servile, fainéant fear is the emotional climate much favored of the idols. Fear them, pay homage, fall into base servitude.

Not so with Jeremiah. Both the idols and their artificers are mocked mercilessly. Truth is, the images are—nothing. And those who concoct them and reverence them—their humanity recedes to the vanishing point.

And what of "the nations," those begetters and purveyors of idolatry? The prophets have much to say of them, and all is in deflation of their pretensions. Yahweh rules the nations. There is "none like Yahweh."

And the sovereign word goes on: "Do not fear them." Into the intellectual and moral wasteland of the idols and their votaries, the word of God concerning who God is, explodes. And of a sudden the truth is in the air—the polluted air of the nations; a world that, left to its own resources, is utterly incapable of the truth or of uttering it or submitting before it.

10:17–22. Probing the source of the nearing tragedy, Jeremiah singles out the "stupid shepherds" and their bereft "scattered flock." The former he all but names: Manasseh and Jehoiakim, the reigning kings. He contemns these highly secular, political entities, weighing fool's gold in the dark.

True, they were anointed as sacred personages to carry on the work of Moses and the Judges. But they have fallen away; they ape foreign potentates. Aping ironically, the emperor of the hated and feared "nation to the north," presently on the move—moving south.

10:23–24. Jeremiah's prayer: to know the "way," the "step" (10:23). A simple, heartfelt expression of limit, creaturehood, boundary. One is not God: one is forbidden to play God. A prayer then: grant self-knowledge, the truth that arises from knowledge of Yahweh.

Is the grace granted otherwise than through suffering? We take note of the soul of Jeremiah, revealed in his prayer. His soul is a mirror that turns inward and outward both, inward in moral clarity, undistorted, unclouded. Then he turns, compassionate and strong, outward to the world. That grace, that God of gifts. Know thyself, know thy world.

"Correct me..." (10:24). A theme consistent with wisdom, and with wisdom literature (Pss. 6:2; 38:2). But "not with anger"; rather with a sense proper to Yahweh's greatness of heart. With a sense, too, that takes in account our fallen estate, the darkness in which we dwell.

10:25 (also Ps. 79:6–7). A rather sour midrash, probably from the time of exile. One notes the irony; the "anger" of Yahweh, from which Jeremiah had sought surcease, here is invoked. The swath reaches far and wide.

Another voice than Jeremiah's, crying out in a far different time, to be sure: let the wrath of Yahweh be tipped and poured out like molten metal, on those who have destroyed us!

Let it be confessed that we are hardly strangers to such a prayer; we wing it in the direction of a God we long for and project with all our hearts—the God of vengeance. An ancient construct to be sure, and a vent for smoldering generational hatreds; recently and appallingly alive in Bosnia and Northern Ireland and elsewhere.

What shall be said in response? Jesus offers a clue, and more—a vision of forgiveness, uttered in extremis: "Father, forgive..."

7
The God of No Answer
(11:1–14:22)

I Plucked You from Egypt,
That Blazing Furnace (11:1–17)

11:3–4 Cursed be anyone who does not heed the words
of this covenant, which I commanded on the day I
brought your ancestors out of the land of Egypt, out
of the blazing furnace.

11:1–12. "Out of the blazing furnace..." A startling, typically Jeremian surprise. The image is an effortless (or so it seems) effusion of a
great poet. It is linked, as though a mere afterthought, to the timeworn
formula: "On the day I brought your ancestors out..." No difficulty
with "the law" as such! His passion is rather to vindicate a religion
of heart and hands, a faith dramatized in works of compassion and
justice.

11:13–14. The delicts, the gods and their shrines, "are as many as
your cities, O Judah,...and as many as the streets of Jerusalem are...
your altars to burn incense to Baal."

The conclusion is ironic—scarcely to be thought irenic! It is addressed to Jeremiah; we have heard it before: "Therefore do not pray
for this people, nor lift up a cry or a prayer for them. I will not listen
when they call to Me because of their disaster." As before, the passage
invites, challenges us: dare to deconstruct the instruction. So doing, we

come up with the wording of an invitation—to do exactly what purportedly is here prohibited. Else, as heretofore suggested, why forbid the intercession in such detail?

11:15–16. This strangely divided Yahweh! Now "this people," a distancing both subtle and cool, has become—"My beloved."

No calculating the wild tides of a heart, shifting at the whim of no moon, but turning and turning about, at the "cry" and "prayer" of Jeremiah on behalf of the delinquents. A cry and prayer, be it noted, explicitly and with considerable heat, that had been forbidden him.

The commentators speak of "misplaced logia" here. The images are two. First of a wayward "beloved," recusant and yet, for all that, weirdly worshipful. "She" has no right to enter Yahweh's precinct; she gives pain to the Holy One. He questions her deviancy and devotion, both. And another image: "The Lord called your name, a green olive tree, beautiful in fruit and form." And for all that favor and beauty, ruin impends: "a great tumult; he has kindled fire in it."

The images strike one as hardly "misplaced" at all. They fit with tragic exactness the prior themes: temple religion reduced to a void without heart; a failing "faith," empty of works. And the acknowledged beauty of a people so beloved, an olive tree, verdant and fruitful—and (if such can be imagined) self-destructing.

Confession, Silence (11:18–12:6)

We encounter the first of the so-called confessions of Jeremiah. One ponders them in awe; they are unprecedented in prophetic literature. Among the great ones not one has offered so impassioned an analysis of his own soul. Jeremiah's is a spirit locked in life-and-death combat, whether with Yahweh, with the worldly powers, or with his own volcanic moods.

The precipitant of the first confession is a plot instigated against his life. Its sworn purpose is the death of the prophet. The plot is undertaken, be it noted, not by enemies or strangers or the powers that be, but by those of his own household, his relatives and friends. He escapes the net; the conspiracy is uncovered in good time—we are not told how or by whom.

Only then, the danger past, does a reaction set in, the shock strike home. The brush with treachery and death brings in its wake a tidal wave of reflection, deep, prolonged, and bitter. He walks the earth now like a Hamlet, somber, inward, sunken in thought.

Or another image: he brings to mind a self-portrait of Rembrandt, or a Job, a "suffering servant," an Isaiah rejected. Transformed, summoned from death, reborn?

For years he has been a vessel of divine truth. Now the cost is totted up. And he is like a dead man walking, an icon of sheer survival, stark evidence of the price exacted for his discipleship.

How can it be, he asks his soul, this betrayal? It is as though the sun had fallen from the sky. Had he not stood on firm ground? Were not friends at hand, to be trusted and turned to with confidence? For years, more or less tranquil of spirit, he hearkened to the word of God and spoke it boldly, in season and out, firmly, lucidly. No palliatives, no easy generalities. The truth, the consequence!

Now "all, all is changed." A shadow has crossed the sun. A sea change. From hearing and speaking the word, he must now endure the word. The word has broken and entered his dwelling, claimed him for its prey. Can it be that doubt has seized his soul? Many have known at one time or another, the like; a rehearsal of death. He dwells in a land of questions and no answers.

Up to the time of betrayal, the word of Yahweh bore an instructive ring; at times even dudgenous, choleric. Tell them this, tell them that; invariably the word was for the sake of "the people." His role was clear: he was to mediate the word, and occasion arising, to fend off the worst of Olympian lightnings, mitigate disasters threatened, plead and cozen on behalf of others. He stood in God's favor, and knew it. He loved his people, was their interlocutor and friend; he would be their redeemer.

But now? Nothing is clear. He must survive in treacherous waters, must question God. Why this gratuitous evil, launched against the just one, himself? Was it not said that the eye of God was upon the fallen sparrow? What then of his near murder—Had God blinked?

12:1–5. Such plaintive, heartbreaking eloquence!

Not to be wondered that G. M. Hopkins has taken up the theme, almost word for word:

> Thou art indeed just, Lord, if I contend
> with thee; but sir, so what I plead is just.
> Why do sinners' ways prosper? and why must
>   disappointment all I endeavor end?
> Wert thou my enemy, O thou my friend,
>   how wouldst thou worse, I wonder, than thou dost
>   defeat, thwart me?

Two demands Jeremiah dares utter. First, a strict verdict of justice against the wicked. And on God's part, an accounting for the recent awful event befalling himself. Whether the first demand was met we are not told. And of the second we are told precious little—and the little unsatisfactory at that.

Such a clairvoyant scrutinizing of his situation, living as he must in a world of frenzy and closure! Jeremiah looks about him; wickedness is firmly planted, "even producing fruit"! It is as though, simple and good of heart as he is, he cannot bring himself to credit the artful gambit of the betrayers. "Why are those who deal in treachery at ease?"

At peace they are, and more: a squalid satisfaction sits easy on them. How serendipitous is evil! And though Yahweh is "far from their mind," a justifying rhetoric never fails them. No stammering; recondite and ready of tongue they are, above all in matters religious.

And Jeremiah turns upon God that glance of a child, and sees— Someone who sees him. Someone reads him like a text, loves him, simple and free and given as he is—exceedingly good, yes great. God's rare dissenter and truth-teller.

On his victimizers he lets fall a glare of scorn and fury. And a wild outcry: let it be done to them as they would do to me—a violent ending! Jeremiah is far from the "Father forgive" of Jesus. (As far distant as ourselves—we the good vengeful Christian warriors.)

In verse 4, the ecological connection is strongly dwelt upon. What in the natural world can be imagined to prosper, when we humans, spoilers all, are so at odds with our vocation—to "walk gently on the earth." And being at odds with nature, so we are in conflict with the God of nature.

A twist of the knife: "...that wickedness of people, our people, who say: 'God sees nothing.'"

This is a God literally, and in more senses than one, of no consequence. Which is to say (the point of view of such a people)—a pleasant, well-mannered agnosticism quite befits. One is reminded of the Athenian shrug that greeted, and dismissed, Paul (Acts 17:22ff.). And in a sense, too, the God of Jeremiah is of little consequence or none; which is to say, indifferent to human behavior, proclaiming no norm, no law.

And then in utmost contrast, the sense of Jeremiah and Jeremiah's Yahweh (and of Jesus), insisting—there is One who judges. And for our part? We see no judgment falling upon the wicked—but a noninterventionary, noninterfering God. Beating at our ears is a thunderous silence, the dreadful silence of God. The crucifixion of the holy, never done with, shadows our history. Of this, less said the better.

The God of Jeremiah might well be named, like the God of Job and of Revelation (and our God as well?)—the God of No Answer. How one longs to come upon even the hint of an explanation! There is none; the mystery of evil stands intact, in history, in the lives of saints. We scan the prophets for whatever light. But the refusal of light stands on page after page, seer after seer, a deliberate, constant omission throughout scripture. No disposition to proffer, even for their own sake, what we seek.

The kings, the high priests, the tyrants raven on. Exile, scorn, physical violence, martyrdom is the lot of the saints. And it is as though in the lamentable matter that torments Job and Jeremiah and the saints of Revelation—"How long O Lord, how long?"—as though the print were to vanish before our eyes. As though page after page were to go mysteriously blank.

And yet, and yet. This peculiar reticence of the divine is by no means to be linked with a kind of Jovian indifference. Least of all, in regard to the fate of one so beloved and faithful as Jeremiah—or Jesus.

Quite to the contrary, and passionately so. The God of Isaiah: "Shall a mother forget the child of her womb? Even should she forget, I will never forget you. See, upon the palms of My hands I have written your name" (49:15, 16). And for us Christians: "Having loved his own who were in the world, he loved them to the end" (John 13:1).

Yet another implication is to be denied strenuously; that God is here reproving Jeremiah (or elsewhere Job) for raising questions concerning human wickedness and the silence of God.

The suffering continues, the sense of abandonment and betrayal.

And as to the divine reaction in face of the passionate queries of the wronged one—Yahweh remains not precisely mum (words are proffered to be sure). But of what import to the afflicted one?

Nothing of reassurance, quite the contrary. Chesterton (in "Ballad of the White Horse"):

> I tell you naught for your comfort
> Yea, naught for your desire
> save that the sky grows darker yet
> and the sea rises higher.

Yahweh's answer is somewhat like that, comfort, but cold indeed: "You have survived thus far. And you will require strength upon strength, to survive greater trials. This is all My word. This, and the assurance offered at the time of your calling—an assurance never once, for all pain and reversal, canceled or withdrawn: 'I will be with you, to protect you.'"

Jeremiah's Diagnosis: A Culture of Sin (12:7–13:27)

12:7–13   "Lament, lament with Me!
         They rant and raven
         and I their prey!

         But yesterday
         a small silly
         birdling they were—
         now hawkish, bestriding
         high heaven,
         intent they are, devouring.

         And earth a shambles!
         Shepherds trampling the vineyards!
         Sowing wheat, reaping thorns—
         harvesters of shame!

Such images of disaster: one is hard put to decide whether the lamentation proceeds from Yahweh or from Jeremiah. Or perhaps as their glance falls upon the fair land in ruins, voice and heart are at one. Mutuality in grief makes of two a single voice, keening a tragic choral ode.

12:14–17. A word now for the neighbors of Judah—a word of reassurance and judgment, much resembling the word to the defaulting chosen. The gentiles are threatened with the fate of Judah: uprooting and exile. Under dire threat, they too must renounce the Baals. Then they, together with the Jews, are invited into the circle of worship.

This accomplished, Judah and the nations alike are heartened by a promise: no more exile to be endured, no more uprooting of Jew or gentile. All will return to their own place.

We have a midrash of note. During or after exile, a scribe has set down a commentary on the preceding "duet," the original oracle of Jeremiah. Now the prophet is presented in a far different light: as a universal, proselytizing voice, in the image of Isaiah (2:1–4; 19:16–25; 56:6–8; 60:11–14) and Micah (4:1–3).

Momentous. Let all, all enter the sanctuary, all ascend the mountain of the Lord!

13:1–27. We come to the first symbolic action exacted of Jeremiah. He is to purchase an article variously described as "underclothing," "waistband," "shorts." He is then to carry the garment some distance toward a river, concealing it in a cleft of rock, thereby exposing the garment to inclement weathers, damp and fog.

And on returning some time later, let him discover (as if he would not know beforehand!) that the vesture is gone rotten. So it shall be with this people. A rather obvious mime or parable?

But wait, something more is at issue here. The garment is suggestive of loving intimacy, designed to be worn close to the loins—as close indeed as a covenant, cherished to the very entrails. Worn close by Jeremiah—or by a people of Yahweh? or both?

But it is not so worn, so cherished; it is abandoned, cast to the rude weathers of the world. What then can be thought to occur? The garment is found soiled, fetid, profitless. Thus do dear things, in a world of folly, go for naught.

Then, the broken wine jars. Now play the fool, Jeremiah, is the inference. Say to them: a wine jar is for wine. And they will answer, exasperated: But who doesn't know that? Put them to silence with this! Shout it like a man gone mad: "To the brim I will fill them all, the kings, the priests, the prophets, the people of Jerusalem—with drunkenness. Then I will shatter them, one against the other, like clay pots breaking to shards!"

(We have seen it in our time, in another, not very different, form: the "Mutually Assured Destruction" of the nuclear arms race. The anagram MAD tells it: those who would break others to pieces, to a nuclear dust. And so purposing, so researching and deploying, are themselves broken; shards of the human.)

13:15–17   Be mindful, give heed
before darkness whelms
you, stumbling about
on mountain wastes crepuscular.

You long for dawn?
    I send you
night
deep as hell's throat, engorging.

You heed me not!
I weep;
     your plight
death upon death multiplied,
My people
a caravan of chattels
pillar to post driven—
wanton the way, witless
strewn with corpses!

13:18–27 Dignity undone—
your kingdom a whoredom—
throne toppled, an interloper
wielding the proud scepter,
barbarians
lording over,

your necks bowed low
chattel, shackled—
hither, yon, on desert winds
scattered, a chaff.

Shall the leopard then
change spots at will?
     Shall you,
evil your wont and will,
beyond custom, become
virtuous on the moment?

The diagnosis is merciless. Jeremiah sees his culture steeped in a "state of sin." Its nearest images are addiction, delusion, atavism, bravado, treachery, brigandage, rapine. Yes, outright murder. He sees as well the consequence of this "sin become of nature," the morally abnormal normalized. He sees catastrophe in the offing.

The calamity is a matter of history: the Babylonian invasion and victory of 605 BCE. But for ourselves, this would seem hardly the point. A larger and looming truth is implied: the go-around that comes around.

Whose God Prevails? (14:1–22)

A drought again, afflicting both landscape and people. Jeremiah composes a formal lamentation; the probable setting is a liturgy of mourning.

The form is typical: question after question is put to Yahweh, in face of disaster. How can God wreak such havoc against his own? (We recall that Jeremiah raised similarly agonized questions when his life was placed in the breach [chap. 12].)

And repeatedly Yahweh has approved such questioning, at least by implication and indirection—as itself a noble form of faith. (And so do we question; and receive not answers, but strength and encouragement—simply to go on.)

Another theme of the liturgical lament: the honor of God at stake. The argument takes this form. If the people, recusant as they are (and willing so to confess), yet subject repeatedly to divine anathema, if these are destroyed by "the nations"—whose god will be said to prevail?

The point is hardly an elevated one. It is as though a canny juridical point were being raised; or a bargaining chip, a quid pro quo, were proffered. That is: Why not, in view of the conflicting claims of the gods, why not simply forgive and forget? Do you, Yahweh, not owe it to yourself, thus to vindicate your sovereignty?

Yet, we think, goodness dwells here too; such "faith," rambunctious and argumentative, implies a robust shouldering aside of second thoughts and enervating doubts, a reliance on God's saving power. Something like: "We are after all no better than we should be; and surely you know it. Forgive then, and forget—you owe it. . . ."

> 14:2–10 From the land, a long
> susurration of grief,
> daylong, nightlong,
> murmurous, the mourning.
>
> Handmaids (command the nobles),
> go fetch us water!
> But of water
> (save of tears)
> there is none—
> skies sere as earth,
> heaven a cracked cistern.

Afield, in the dust,
a doe gives birth
atremble, wanders away
disconsolate,
her faun's first breath
its last.

On barren heights
wild donkeys bray,
distressed, panting like jackals.

And you, Yahweh,
our hope firm planted
our Strength and Savior—
why then, why?

Are you then
   a Stranger
approaching, passing
yonder, elsewhere—
a shrug for our plight?

Daring, daunting images indeed! Shall we speak even of—Jeremian taunts? No emollient people these; and he no amiable clone, mouthing platitudes on their behalf. None such. But an uncowed people and their prophet, he gifted with verbal artifice and sprightly tongue.

Still for all that, Yahweh remains unmoved. (For the moment, it must be added.) His riposte is far from encouraging. Shall he yield, entreated as he is to cast his accusations aside, to cancel transgressions, when to the present moment, despite all protestations to the contrary, the crimes continue to fester?

Yahweh takes note of the Jeremian prayer; the answer is in the negative.

Then an instruction to the prophet; we have heard it before. These are words whose true import lies deep, contradicts or "deconstructs" the literal sense. At the start, Yahweh is stormily resolved (but only at the start) on the annihilation of this wicked tribe. The decision is irrevocable (but not really). Once more therefore Jeremiah is strictly forbidden (but not really) to intercede.

In this matter we, to be sure, are in a favored position; we have at hand the entire book of Jeremiah. And as the narrative unrolls, it becomes clear that the worst did not occur—only the worse. The apocalyptic outcome was averted; the people were not exterminated. They were driven in exile. But they survived to return.

And what of those imperial tormentors, arrogant, seemingly omnipotent, driving their victims before them?

Astonishing. They are vanished, no more than a reference, a footnote to biblical history. Minor players in a drama whose protagonists and heroes are—those they tormented and enslaved.

Thus went the threats and fulminations of Yahweh: they were uttered; they were not fulfilled. And we have for our instruction a gift beyond measure: Jeremiah the intercessor, ardent and unfailing, this martinet and lover. Not giving up, not despairing (of his own or his God), speaking up, daring to disobey the (on the face of it) rude command: once for all, cease and desist!

Heart's thanks to you, Jeremiah, painfully spinning from your guts a classic (and yes, divinely sanctioned) "history from below." For offering so great a gift to the unborn. Our prophet, speaking for us.

14:14–17. Other voices than Jeremiah's raise a clamor.

Their din is reassuring to the thoughtless. They would allay projected fears and dreads. Their urging: pay no heed to this armageddonist, Jeremiah. There will be no war, no famine; only peace in our time!

The message is an outright lie, and Yahweh is indignant. "Falsehood, and in My name! I have neither sent them nor commanded them nor spoken to them." And again, these seers see nothing of the truth, but "a false vision, divination, futility, and the deception of their own minds."

The passage is curiously repetitive. It is as though Yahweh were ruminating within himself, unable quite to credit his hearing. On a scene of impending disaster, only atavism and futility thrive; a tawdry band of hallucinators buzz about, deceiving and disorienting the people.

These offer no critique of political realities, no reproof, no urge to repent. Instead, they busily shore up the corrupt, unjust system on which they have staked all. Talk about acculturated religion!

An instruction is implied, a hard lesson: when God raises up a true prophet, the false foregather. Thus is implied a primary law of the Fall: in such a world as ours, the truth never goes unopposed. The truthteller is a "dramatis persona," more, the protagonist of the drama. As such, Jeremiah will be required to pay up, dearly.

For in every such encounter, an antagonist lurks.

Jeremiah has already begun payment: the threat of death, hovering over his pronouncements. Are we rash in concluding that the "untruth-tellers" are those who earlier sought his death? Whether or not such a connection can be made, the moral linkage is clear. Jeremiah and his kind (Jesus and his kind) must be put to silence—the ultimate silence of death.

Thus the law of the Fall is enacted.

14:17–22   Night and day, lamentation
eyes blind with tears
for the mortal hurt of my people!

The verdant countryside
stagnant, stinking with corpses;
the holy city
stricken heel to eye,
a vast cenotaph.

Summon prophet and priest?
No faith, no comforting.

Have You then rejected us,
beyond heal-all
in loathing stricken us?

For your Name's sake
recall the promise,
your covenant—that love
unstinting, forfending!

The text is another formal lament. First, an agonized questioning of God: How can such horrors befall? And then, the invoking of God's honor: "For your name's sake, recall the covenant."

8
I, Jeremiah, Child of Contention and Strife (15:1–20:18)

Yahweh: "Plead No More for Them" (15:1–21)

15:1–4. Yet once more, O ye laurels!

Again an urgent, stubborn resolve, a threat underscored by Yahweh as irrevocable. (And yet as so often before, the threat was revoked, at least in degree!)

Yahweh speaks; and we note how his word to a favorite son goes counter to the initial calling. In the beginning, Jeremiah was summoned to intercede. Here he is told once more, and sternly, to plead no more. The command is uttered in all seriousness—What could be thought more final? "Could you summon those Great Intercessors, Moses and Samuel, I would turn a deaf ear. Even to them. So why not to you?'

Dismissal most abrupt.

The two are honored in the tradition, great and skilled mediators between a jealous God and a recusant people, the Rock and the hard of heart (Exod. 32:11–14; Num. 14:11–25; 1 Sam. 7:5–9; 12:19–23). And one is led to wonder: Is Jeremiah here considered as falling short of their stature? Hardly. Let history tell.

Then begins a hypothetical, truly awful exchange. Yahweh to Jeremiah: "Tell them [the people] to go away, to leave my presence. And when they ask [one senses the anguish and dislocation that fuels the question of a demoralized people], 'Where then shall we go?'—answer this: 'Go to your death—by disease, famine, sword, exile.'" A text that burns in the mind. Pure terror, fury, rejection.

It burned also in the mind of the author of Revelation (13:9–10). He locates the words of Jeremiah in his own time and place: the era of the Beast, the Roman Empire, and the "defeat" of the saints. In one sense everything is new; in another nothing is new. Different victimizer, different victim to be sure.

But as to method, one and the same: the misdeeds of an earlier fearsome bestial regime, then a later. The Roman tyrant apes in bloody jot and tittle, the Babylonian. And the response of the community? "This calls for endurance and faith on the part of God's people" (Rev. 13:10).

It is worth noting too that in Revelation, the Jeremian text is freed of its oppressive, threatening overtone. In the Christian midrash, no angry Yahweh fulminates. Rather, a matter-of-fact statement is presented; its basis is the life and death of Jesus, and the mimetic vocation of the believers.

Thus the earlier text is transformed. Borrowing the awful words of Jeremiah, the author of Revelation simply issues a manifesto of the Christian vocation. To wit: hear this. In face of the powers of the world, "those destined for death, will go to death." Which is to say, there is a bloody logic, an inevitability even, implied in discipleship. Given the world's juridical weaponry, and given the intractable faith of the early community, a clash is inevitable: law vs. conscience.

Violent death is decreed for the nonviolent. The saints perish, the Beast prevails—for awhile.

Yahweh, Jeremiah, Jerusalem: a trinity of anguish and lamentation. First, Yahweh lingers in mourning for the city, much beloved, guilty as its people are. And doomed:

> 15:5, 8 Who then takes pity
> on rose-red Jerusalem
> blood-red, heart-red once—
> gone to gray ash
> bowed to earth
> in sackcloth and filth?...
>
> Widows numerous
> mothers bereft

> their sun at noonday
> quenched utterly...

Then Jeremiah takes up the dirge on his own behalf:

> 15:10 O my mother
>   why did you bear me
>   breathing into the world,
>   child of contention and strife?

And mother Yahweh speaks:

> 15:10 Tenderly my son
>   I bore you
>   breathing into the world
>   all, all to good cause;
>   intercessor, suppliant
>   voice of the voiceless....

And Jeremiah:

> 15:16–18 Yahweh,
>   You touched my lips
>   set them afire, set me apart—
>   *saeva indignatio*...
>
>   You, my
>   Wound unhealed
>   for offspring, for portion
>   for harvest, yes tenfold
>   for Lover,
>   You,
>   You my glory.
>
>   See, proud I wear You,
>   a wedding ring,
>   pure gold, fired
>   in furnace of love!
>
>   Your word my nectar,
>   I quaff it, wax strong—
>   You, joy to my heart
>   valor of limb!

And Yahweh to Jeremiah, weighty with instruction:

I, Jeremiah, Child of Contention and Strife (15:1–20:18)   73

15:19, 20–21   Before me, stand.
            Choose the good, reject dross.
            This people, mayhap
            a willy, a nilly
            turn, turn not
            hearken, or not—
            but you, turn
            turn to me only!…

            You firm set
            as a bronze stele—
            see, I plant you,
            no one
            ever, anon to
            supplant
            you!

Jeremiah: His Life a Lonely Cry in the Night (16:1–21)

Jeremiah is commanded not to marry, to forgo offspring. Such a difficult vocation, and hardly to be thought unusual. Celibacy—a harsh staple of the prophetic calling. No love but God's! Like the thrust of a blade Yahweh enters, invading and claiming the dark declivities of life.

Examples abound. Hosea must undertake a marriage bound to turn out badly (chaps. 1–3). Ezekiel's wife dies of no specified illness; she simply is made to disappear. And another awful stipulation: the prophet, abruptly and unaccountably bereft, is forbidden to mourn (24:15–27).

So to Jeremiah the word is, no marriage, no family. This despite the cultural sense, ancient as Genesis, that a large progeny marks God's blessing (22:17; Ps. 127:3, 4). More, sterility is considered a curse (Gen. 30:1; 1 Sam. 1:6–8). And such virginity as is here enforced is hardly respected; rather, it is an occasion for mourning (Judg. 11:37).

Are we to think of Jeremiah's bachelorhood as a quasi-symbol? It would seem so, with heavy dramatic overtones. And perhaps a touch of irony as well. We note the pit of loneliness into which he is hurled repeatedly. And all the while, his boundless capacity for love! a heart large and valiant and vigilant for the well-being of his own. A heart, one is tempted to add, that dares challenge Yahweh, crying out, on occasion even rebuking. Risking thereby divine fury (never slow to descend)!

His single estate, then, is hardly to be considered (by us, by himself) an unmixed blessing. Yet, unmarried and childless, he will be spared the fate of others, both adults and children. He will survive, while many are marked for violent death. (Survival a blessing? But what can this mean, when one's world is reduced to a vast ossuary?)

The divine anger blazes, white hot. Not only extermination of the living is decreed; burial is denied the dead. Appalled, we witness the final revenge against an unheeding, churlish people. And Jeremiah, no spouse or child to mourn, moves amid the calamities like a zombie, a stalking corpse.

(Vengeance of Yahweh? Perhaps. At the same time one senses the anguished double mind of Jeremiah, who can scarce enter into such a mood. Vengeance? No. He is after all, not God.) Yet is Jeremiah not an evidence of the double mind of Yahweh—a spirit of eye-for-eye contested by a heart welling with maternal love?

Why otherwise, the choice of so opposite a temperament, to speak for Yahweh—even as the prophet opposes him?

Who, then, one wonders, can be thought to speak for God? God—subject to this mood or that; or Jeremiah—the two being so often harshly in contention? (And to speak of ourselves, pondering the book and its complexities, Whom of these two are we advised to emulate, to obey, to adhere to? Deep matters.)

Did Jeremiah follow through? Did he obey what must have appeared a further assault on his human and religious longings? First wife and children are denied him. Then, mourning for the dead is forbidden. No mark of grief on his person, no "gashing himself or shaving his head." No part in ceremonies of lamentation, no "breaking of bread," no "cup of consolation." A stoic prophet, detached, indifferent?

For his part, and up to the present episode, Yahweh has been faithful to the initial promise: "You will be like a fortified city, an iron pillar, and a bronze wall."

And yet, and yet. When Jeremiah is allowed to speak, the text falls to the page like tears. His heart is worn on his sleeve; his life is like a cry in the night. Whether he would agree that such similes, "fortified city, iron pillar, bronze wall," did him honor, corresponded well with his sensibility, his "way of the heart"—this perhaps remains moot.

16:9. The fall of Jerusalem. And despite all, the eye of Yahweh lingers in loving detail upon the scene of loss: no more "the voice of rejoicing and the voice of gladness; the voice of the bridegroom and the voice of the bride." Another, later seer will borrow the words, an image heartrending and precise, of the fall of great Babylon (Rev. 18:23).

16:10–13. Yahweh summons Jeremiah, sets the scene. Talk about close encounters!

Jeremiah is reminded once more in a dramatic dialogue: he is a mouthpiece of the Holy, word for word, jot and tittle.

The people are offstage. Only imagine: this they will say to you; this you will answer. No laissez-faire here, little or nothing allowed of improvisation or spontaneity.

The people speak: "What have we done, that Yahweh is angry?"

Jeremiah, baldly: "The sin is idolatry; it is in your bloodstream, in your behavior. Therefore, exile is decreed. Spiritually at odds, off kilter, exiled from the truth of life as you are—banishment will mount, a public drama of the lamentable inner reality."

In Jeremiah's lifetime, we are informed, Yahweh was conceived as a "local God," presumed to dwell only in Israel. Yet the anomaly: the tribe is to be "thrown," as here is threatened, "out of this land, into a land which neither you nor your ancestors have known." It will then follow that "you will serve other gods day and night" (1 Sam. 26:19).

One is allowed to infer a meaning deeper than that of a partially developed monotheism. Which is to say, the war of myths, conflict between service of Yahweh and service of false gods, has been underway for a long time—and in the heartland, in Jerusalem and the temple worship enacted there. The "kings and priests and prophets and people," all classes previously indicted, are already "serving other gods day and night." Thus Yahweh can logically add, as though the abominations were before him (which they surely are), "...and I will show you no mercy."

And yet despite all provocation, Yahweh is not done with mercy. An unquenchable echo of the heart hints, in spite of present follies, at other behaviors and possibilities. Yes. Even on our part. Hope beats on, the heartbeat of God. And mercy reasserts itself, another name of the living God.

We follow in Yahweh the uneasy path of logic and illogic, of mind in sole command, and heart outspoken. Each is heard from, a tempestuous interior monologue, as Yahweh ponders: What is to be done with this truculent, unmanageable tribe? It is as though Jeremiah, the suffering servant, were ever-present, silent, hovering there, his pleas unspoken. He is appointed and anointed, but by no means in view of subservience. He will be heard from.

His vocation: to be an "opposite number," someone to be reckoned with, even by God. To read the heart, vulnerable and changeful, of Yahweh. And to respond.

Jeremiah stands in the forefront of the few great ones who "correct" Yahweh. Which is to say (and of necessity to say clumsily)—regarding the truth of Yahweh, Jeremiah is beset by far fewer inhibitions, projections, illusions perennially nurtured, than are the "kings and priests and prophets, and people." He knows Yahweh, a fearsome statement. And he pays the price attached to dangerous knowledge.

Further: the Yahweh he knows would have him tell the truth—first of all concerning Yahweh. Thus underway is a tremendous wrestling match—between the Yahweh hucstered by the priests, and the Yahweh of Jeremiah's visionary heart—his capacity for truth and tenderness, both. He must wrestle the dark angel nightlong. And like Jacob, he emerges from the fray, wounded.

Another truth (the same really, but from a different angle). He is to tell the truth about "this people." Unpalatable, outrageous! The truth: they have gotten (begotten) god(s) of their dark desire.

Further. This is the description of their pantheon. The Baals are in large part imported from the nations. They are bereft of transcendence; violent and vengeful, they act as guardians of the dominant culture. They befit and cozen the instincts, their greed and violence. So doing, they mirror, enhance, enlarge the appetitive ego. Thus they enslave, creating in place of community, a slave quarters, a corral for a "collective."

Then enters Jeremiah, correcting, reproving, purifying, rebuking. And paying dear: undergoing in himself the consequence of a difficult, all-but-impossible vocation. A vocation whose near impossibility was spelled out from the beginning by Yahweh.

Thus, one thinks, such scenes as this—verses 14 and 15. Yahweh ruminating, then self-correcting. Because of Jeremiah, because of Yahweh's great love for Jeremiah? In any case, under whatever softening influence, Yahweh himself utters a midrash, mitigating once more the fury of an earlier decree. He will have a new title (self-conferred?) in consequence of a new chapter here underway.

Remember, my people, remember!—the cry. Exile in Egypt was a stage, an episode of your history, rather than a permanent immersion in loss and defeat. For you stood free once more, returned, recovered your land. So too it shall be with Babylon, this loss and defeat and banishment. It will be marked by another "great return."

And Yahweh will glory in a title that celebrates yet another munificent act: your Savior.

16:16–20. First, a vivid image of the invasion mounted against the (would-be) empire, Jeremiah's own land. For a prelude, fishermen and hunters are dispatched on what amounts to a "search and destroy" mission. And the prey of this fierce image? The perennially abominated idolaters.

The language is relentlessly clear: the idols are "lifeless as corpses." It is as though the hunters, following a spoor, come only on a dead prey; the "worshipers" are already perished. Thus the drama, instead of a climax, reaches only a dead-end—an image of the lifelessness of such lives.

The thunderations of Yahweh are like a recitative, uttered in the presence of Jeremiah. He must be thought to respond. And as is typical of his spirit, canny and wild and yet so lucid, he takes to heart both the threat and the pause. Then, as though with a gesture of love, he turns the thrust aside.

He utters a prayer, and more than a prayer—a graceful implied cosseting of angry Yahweh. First: "You it is who give me strength and help in time of trouble." Then, regarding the idolaters: "They abominate, yes, but let us ever so gently widen the issue, grant it a fortunate outcome, and thus defuse your fury."

Thus Jeremiah has a prophecy of his own, offered to comfort Yahweh: one day, the idolatries of all the ages will come to a halt. And more: the devotees will confess and repent and arrive at a better heart, converted to true God: "Nations will come to you from the ends of the earth."

We might have expected such words, but proceeding only from Yahweh. No, they are Jeremiah's, his daring. In a Godlike moment of clairvoyance (and tact!), he takes visionary words to himself. It is exactly what needs saying—exactly, one thinks, what Yahweh longs to hear.

The last day—this is the key to the heart of the Creator! Jeremiah assembles the actors, outlines the script and action. The idolaters know a change of heart; the idols are broken. The truth at last prevails. Jeremiah is vindicated, his long patience. Yahweh also, that long impatience.

One and the same triumph, all said.

16:21. And to all intents, Yahweh agrees. One imagines the deific One nodding approval. And growing calm, in the assurance of Jeremiah; Yahweh remains, despite all pretenders to the throne, Yahweh. "I am going to make them know My power and might."

This oneiric, judicious Jeremiah is master of the right word, mover in the needful direction!

Clay in the Potter's Hand (17:1–19:15)

17:1–4   With iron stylus
no; diamond point
your sin is engraved,
a wound, a mortal thrust
to My heart
    stopped
in midbeat.
Sin. Scored,
hammer and chisel, alpha—
omega, on altar stone.

False altars, raised
to no living god, to no good—
nor yours nor Mine.

Retribution Mine!
A coven of furies
seize, scatter to four winds
you, useless, chaff!

17:5–8 Thus Yahweh:
    cursed the one
whose trust
stops short of Me,
    lodged
foolish, futile
in humankind,
who Me
belittle, of Me
make near nothing!

Rootless, blind,
weightless, sterile,

that one—
a tumbleweed
by vagrant winds
buffeted
hither and yon.

Not that one!
Blessed the one
whose hope takes root
deep, deep in Me.

A waterfall, soft
as ghost's footfall
rewards the root
planted firm, ever green—

Hope on, hope on,
in due time, yes
plenteous My harvest!

17:13–14, 18   You. Our sole hope!
Fountain, Living Water.
Those who forsake You—
their names writ in dust
dust shall be, and no more.

   Heal me then—
healed I shall be.
   Save me—
on the moment, saved....

Dies Irae!
In days of dread
You: refuge and relief.

17:19–27. Another last-ditch try; Jeremiah is dispatched on a lengthy preaching mission. He is to stand at every gate of Jerusalem, uttering an admonition as to sabbath observance. The passage seems uncharacteristic, in its rather dry solemnity. (No need to add—every word of the passage has been dustily and learnedly scrutinized, as to time and author.)

It seems plausible that we have an original oracle, modified by a midrash. In any case, Jeremiah is echoing a very old legislation, dating from Exodus and Deuteronomy. The prohibition against "carrying of burdens" is stern: "as you love your lives." Observance of the day of rest is presented as a practical, manageable tribute to Yahweh Creator—and by implication, to the dignity of observant humans. Stop all ordinary routine, getting and spending and laboring and chattering away. Take breath, take heed, grow mindful.

18:1–12. More familiar, characteristic terrain: Jeremiah and Yahweh, the image-makers. And another task assigned: Jeremiah is instructed to visit the workshop of a potter.

There he observes a mass of clay, an intended vessel, failing to take shape on the wheel, then falling to pieces. But no great loss—the potter tries again; he gathers and reworks the clay, with a better outcome.

A dramatic parable: "Behold, as the clay is in the potter's hand, so you are in My hand, O house of Israel." Yahweh the potter; beautiful certainly, consoling—perhaps. We shall see. And we the clay: an ancient image, recalling the story of the Original Week and the creation of the first parent (Gen. 2:7), a theme taken up repeatedly by Isaiah (29:16; 45:9; 64:7).

The potter works freely; he takes the clay in hand one time, many times; whatever is required to repair and remake the spoiled pot. So God is free—to alter this or that decree.

The image works two ways: a decree of doom may be altered by conversion of the human heart. Or when evil deeds betray a promise made, the decree of blessing may be changed to a curse.

The changes rung here echo instructions given Jeremiah at the start (1:10): "I have appointed you this day over the nations. To pluck up and break down. To destroy and to overthrow. To build and to plant." In the beginning, the work is underscored as Jeremiah's own; now the same work is declared to be Yahweh's.

Harsh language, and unmistakably clear. In each instance the first task—the first word—is a naysaying. No toleration, no minor (or even major!) adjustment of an inherently wicked, inhuman system. The "no" precedes the "yes," in the nature of things. What sort of dwelling can be built on rotten foundations?

One notes too that the images of "no" are more detailed than those of "yes": "to pluck up, break down, destroy, overthrow." No mistaking the intent—to start over, to grant nothing of legitimacy or place to a discredited system.

More: the "no" is included and presupposed in the "yes." The primary "no" gives to the final "yes" ("to build up, to plant") its dignity, seriousness, and weight.

I, Jeremiah, Child of Contention and Strife (15:1–20:18)

(Let us however avoid extremism. Let us speak of "good" nuclear weapons; good because ours. And of evil ones, brandished by our enemies.

(Let us wage only "just" wars; just because waged by us.

(Let us approve ROTC on Catholic campuses; correctly approved because the students are Catholic, marching under a religious vexilla.

(Let us sanction and honor Christian military chaplains; they after all bring aid and comfort to Christian warriors.)

In other words, let no prophetic "no" be uttered in face of worldly systems of captivation and control, of morbidity and slack morality. Let us "go with what goes." Let us honor the empire with an unmodified, unmitigated, spiritless, spineless "yes."

18:13–17   Who has heard the like?
            My people turn, turn away.

            Are the Himalayan heights
            denuded of snow?
            Do mountain streams in flood
            run dry?

            But My people—
            they turn, turn away
            afoul of the good path
            into bramble, thicket, wasteland.
            Lost they are.
                From them, see—
            I too
                turn, turn away.

18:18–23. Trouble again, for Jeremiah.

What a threat this good man has become—to everyone, it would seem, even to those entrusted with the wisdom of the tribe. What in his message rubs them raw? Up to the present instance, we are hardly told. But perhaps the node of the conflict can be inferred, at least in general terms. From the beginning the word of God has urged upon him a message of upheaval, a rejection of useless forms of religion and wicked behavior.

In face of the social situation, there are weighty reasons for keeping silence. Special interests, laws of primogeniture, vestiges of honors anciently conferred—these are at stake. Does he then dare include in his denunciations the priests and their teaching (torah), the prophetical word (*dabar*), the sages and their counsel (*esa*)? He does, beyond doubt. Each and all, these eminences are called in question.

No wonder the sky falls in on the naysayer! No wonder a barrage of antipathy erupts!

Hard falls the message.

They, the guardians, even the artisans of public weal, are to be removed. And whatever is raised on the rubble of their malfeasance, is to be placed in other hands than theirs; the form of the future will hardly accord with their notions or ambitions. Their power is canceled; once for all, their line is broken. It is Jeremiah and his like, not they and theirs, who will "build up," and "plant."

Inferred as to our plight and task is Peter Maurin's urging to "create the new in the shell of the old." A birth impending—with bloodletting and tears implied in the metaphor. And in other lands and times, a bloody assault is launched against believers.

We have lived to see it: in Guatemala and Nicaragua and El Salvador the Jeremian community has faced a policy of torture, disappearance, the slaughter of the innocents.

The point would be simply to "create the new" by living the new. A better law, that of love; a purer wisdom; hope and compassion in abundance. Freedom from the nagging demons of violence, healing of hardened hearts.

Here and there in our world, these moral splendors are at hand— thanks to the remnant, the communities of resistance. And but for these, a moral wasteland stretches far and wide, with little or no relief: the culture of death.

Who would claim that our saint and savant is altogether shriven of the spirit of vengeance, that Jeremiah does not harbor instincts of "getting even," does not entreat Yahweh to "avenge his wrongs"?

Indeed his moods are complex, at times contradictory. He blows hot, blows cold; like Yahweh, like Yahweh's man! More: his summoning of Yahweh to hasten to judgment reveals the darkness that lurks in the noblest of hearts. Reveals much too concerning his understanding, the projection of his image—of Yahweh. Darkness within and without.

Who is this God anyway, the God of Jeremiah, what of his moral physiognomy? Do such oracles as are here recorded, with their summons to violent reprisal (a call taken seriously, more, initiated again and again by Yahweh), offer sound insight into God, our God as well as Jeremiah's? Insight into God's hope for ourselves? into crime (ours) and punishment (God's)—an ineluctable hyphenation, a logic of terrifying consequence?

Why does the God of Jeremiah never once counsel—forgiveness?

For this we are forced to turn in another direction than Jeremiah, to a later time, another seer—maligned as he is, put to scorn, murdered. And amid the infamy, a far different response is offered his persecutors; a prayer on their behalf, an intercession (Luke 23:24).

Jeremiah, we confess in confusion of heart, much resembles ourselves. And Jesus much resembles God. But not the God of Jeremiah; the God of Jesus.

19:1–14. It is the old story of idolatry, once more dramatized, the action suiting, illuminating the word. Jeremiah is instructed to procure a flask. Then in company of elders and priests, he is to proceed to a gate of the city. And before witnesses, to break the clay vessel in pieces.

The "clay," as Genesis suggests, is the "prime matter" of creation. A prior episode took the story further (18:1ff.). That clay, we were told, was soft upon the wheel. If the potter failed, he could try again, the breaking-remaking sequence suggesting the possibility of conversion. Once that occurred, one could infer a corresponding change of heart in Yahweh. He too is "converted": from threat to welcoming love.

Here the message is hardly as comforting. The clay is no longer malleable; it was lifted from the wheel and baked hard in a kiln. So its form, good or ill, is final. Now it illustrates only one outcome, an awful one at that. Jeremiah is told: do it. Break the vessel in shards. For the people, the message is dire; devastation is your fate.

The point has been made at the gate, referring to the secular order. Now the drama is to be repeated in the court of the temple. The sin is one, hyphenated—idolatry-injustice. And here both powers are indicted, religious and secular.

The Rub: False Worship (20:1–18)

As to the civil reaction, no hint is given. But the temple authorities! They are wounded to the quick; on the instant they retaliate.

The psychology here implied (not to make much of little) is of some interest. We suppose that Jeremiah was allowed to speak freely at the city gate; he spoke up, and no penalty was imposed. Perhaps he was received with indifference, no credit being accorded his predictions.

In any case, he finished his speech unimpeded and turned
the temple, there to repeat his fractious words.

And the sky falls in. The religious leadership grows furi
seer, hallucinating and peevish as he is, must pay up, and d
order of the chief priest he is whipped and taken in custody. The
place of detention is variously described: "stocks," a "holding tank,"
a "prison," a "cramped room."

It is the first recorded arrest of Jeremiah, but hardly the last, as will
appear (37:13).

And why, we wonder, the marked contrast in the reaction of the
powers? Why the equivalent shrug by the secular authorities, the swift
punishment meted out by the religious? One thinks of the skin, thin
as a gold leaf, that quivers away beneath a public patina of religiosity
and respectability.

The repeated, burning accusation of "false worship" raised by Jeremiah seems to be the rub. His diatribe touches on extremely practical
matters—such matters (Need one add?) as were best left raised.

(Such matters will seldom if ever be raised by those who stand
within the circle of domination. Nor will like matters be raised by
the authorities of the state. For them, certain providers of religion are
steadying comrades indeed.)

Let us here and now grasp the nettle. One thinks of such matters as
misuse of money, special interests and immunities, high-riding egos,
and sundry other accusations harped on by Jeremiah and his Yahweh, including maltreatment and contempt shown the poor. Shall one
take note in sum, as do the accusers, of the considerable gap between
virtuous words and questionable moral practice?

As to the last-mentioned matter (and perhaps the entire list of de-
viances), the temple coterie must be accounted a sedulous ape of the
state potentates. With this caveat, as made necessary by the speedy
punishment that befell the prophet: the temple crew is far more sen-
sitive to a prophetic word. Its bad faith, thus unveiled, is the more
speedily inflamed. But the two, in effect and intent, comprise a single
power—like a crutch and a cripple, each walking a crooked mile.

Talk about an unbroken spirit! No sooner released, the following
morning Jeremiah (19:3ff.) proceeds to tongue-lashing the priest who
has punished him. Nothing daunted, no least thought of blunting the
truth, of having "learned his lesson'!

He calls to mind other noble defendants in history, Jesus before Pilate, and the apostles of the early church, hauled before the religious

authorities of that time and place. The common thread of faithful behavior suggests a common determination: a "justice system," untruthful, irksome, capricious, morally dilapidated, tedious to right thought—this bogus system, a principality of puppetry, must, if only once, hear the truth concerning itself.

The truth-telling of Jeremiah and of countless others, including the resisters of our own lifetime—is simply an act of love. To the ethically bankrupt judges and prosecutors and jailers, they offer a gift and grant; access to the truth.

Jeremiah confronts the temple claque in much the way of Amos (c.7,vv.1–10). With this difference: Jeremiah dares confer a name on his tormentor. He calls him, and how rightly, "Terror on every side."

It is the inner meaning, the "omen," of Pashur's *nomen*.

As he, the chief priest, has been a terrorizer of the helpless, he shall be terrorized. And Jeremiah proceeds to utter, in eldritch detail, the fate of the supernumerary.

It is as though up to the advent of the prophet, a dark magic has been at work, stifling on the tongue a certain forbidden word: a name, a nation. But Jeremiah is no captive to magic and its dreads and darkness. Let it be spoken, a portent. For the first time, Jeremiah utters the name of the invader—Babylon.

20:7–18   Yahweh, you trickster,
with a flick of your finger
you whirl me about—
this way, that, a weather—
vane in your wild weathers,
whim, tornado, mood.

Never shall I countenance
this mad charade of yours!

You wound me, spur my flanks—
I must
under your whip
a cowering beast
neigh, whinny, roar—
"Root up, Tear down!"
On every side
ridicule greets me,
distain, scorn.

In corners they gather,
like whispering spiders
weaving rumors—
"Malcontent, he sees
through a glass, darkness only."

Friends grown sly,
weave their spells—
"Only wait,
await his downfall!"

My soul beleaguered
whispers:
   Peace, poor soul, peace—
let pass this awful
behest of His
in sweet forgetting!

Then
I swear it
your word erupts—
a fire shut in my bones
smolders there, consuming—
I cannot contain, endure it!

Cursed, thrice cursed
be the ill-starred
night of my birth,
a mother's womb my tomb!
Cursed the gladdening word—
"A child is born, a son!"

Good news?
   No. A plague—
sorrow, disgrace my lot.

Nevertheless,
   You
cloud of unknowing,
of undoing—
I cling to You, fiery pillar cling to You, burn of you
and I sing, I raise
a song against the night;

my Scandal
my Love—
stand with me in the breach!

Interventions, contradictions!

Among the prophets Jeremiah seems to me the most "modern" of sensibilities, kin to the wager of Paschal, Kierkegaard's bleak isolation and abandonment, Hopkins's dark night. Let us dare say, kin to Graham Greene's: "My salvation is: I do not believe my disbelief."

A suffering servant indeed, in harmony with the suffering spirits of our history. Yet by no means is he put to silence—neither by guile, treachery, the mendacity or spleen of the envious.

Never does he equate silence with faith itself—as though faith counseled fatalism or resignation before proliferating injustice, the wrongs to be set right (perhaps, perhaps not) in some "afterlife."

Jeremiah will have none of this; he is kin, in a classical (and largely neglected) sense, to Job, the great here-and-now questioner of God. And to the martyrs of Revelation and their plangent outcry (6:10).

To speak of ourselves, for the most part: we read and run. Yet even we, bystanders, spectators of a terrible drama, are moved beyond words. Shall we be purged of pity and terror?

Jeremiah all but drowns in a torrent of (Dare we describe his plight, who have never undergone anything remotely like it?) stormy moods, the stern demands of—providence. An overseeing so improvident! Yahweh abandons the afflicted one to a dark judgment that, in obedience, he himself has loosed on the world.

What he has loosed on the world is a wild recognition scene. He holds before the powers of the world a mirror. It is merciless. Let the mighty take a close look, at an all-but-unbearable image—of themselves. Of a "something," an undead, a face unmasked, a Mr. Hyde of dark desire and ethos. A victim and victimizer, riding the demons of night.

The images recur, relentlessly. A dark root must be "pulled up," a structure—venerable and honored though it be—must be "pulled down." Is the world fallen from grace and favor? Is it at odds with the world's Creator, at odds with itself? Is the world at odds with the world's people? Has it become the enemy of life and the living? Is the world in fact a "system" at odds with the ecology, moral and physical, of creation?

Is the leopard summoned to change its spots?

The outcome of such relentless truth-telling is predictable (as might be thought, especially by spectators!). It is nonetheless catastrophic. Jeremiah shortly comes to know that "other side" of official benignity, which smiles in tigrish fashion when smiled upon; but shows fang and claw to the interfering.

It is precisely at this point, a time of incessant darkness, that Jeremiah meets our lives, a brother standing at our side. We recognize his cry; it has issued from our own distress. The vesture and gesture of the centuries, the diverse cultures—all dissolve. A terrible beauty is born and born again; Jeremiah and ourselves stand in the same world, our situation strangely like his; our calling as well.

And we note with a kind of transfixed awe that the revulsion is all the more abrupt when the truth in fact offers an only hope. Defeat burns like a seer's "fire" in our bones; Jeremiah's life and ours, his bones and ours, are kindling sticks for the Kristalnacht of the world.

Jeremiah knows it, as we are called to know it. Nothing for it, nothing to be done, except to "keep at it." The truth, despised, put to scorn though it be, remains the truth. It urges. It must be spoken. It sets lives afire. His critique of the world's ways, "Part 1" of the word of Yahweh, offers an innuendo of the Fall, and of the consequence of that event—as it touches perennially, like a finger of Death pointed and personified, individuals and structures.

The critique also implies a task assigned to the believing community. (The sole advantage accruing to such a community, itself fallen, being its archimedean lever—faith.)

The task: the truth concerning the Fall must be spoken in every generation, since in every generation an unrepentant world acts out anew, by rites of domination and exclusion and outright murder, the ancient same criminal drama.

The plight, its consequence. And our vocation as well, and the world's. If it but knew.

And a gift is offered for our edification and instruction, perhaps a prayer taken from his lips and given to ours.

The burden too heavy, the word consequential in "a world too much with us":

> 20:7 You are stronger than I,
>   and You have overpowered me.
>   I am perpetually ridiculed and scorned
>   because I proclaim Your message....

9
Kings and Prophets:
One Morality for All
(21:1–24:10)

Now a transition. (This section is considered a unit, dealing as it does with kings and prophets.)

Mammon and Mars Come Calling (21:10–22:30)

21:1–10. It seems inevitable—the high priests and Jeremiah perennially at odds. So we have yet another confrontation, with a different Pashur. The priest arrives on the scene, pacifically, as one presumes, to consult with the prophet. But the peace will hardly hold; this priest too will shortly show his colors in a splenetic burst of opposition (38:1ff.).

The episode reeks with the self-interest of altitudinous noses, sniffing the winds of chance. Which is to say, now and again it accrues to the advantage of those in power to make use of the likes of Jeremiah. As in the present episode.

Hardly to be thought of single mind, or devoted to the words of the prophet or the God he invokes, such eminences seek to bend the prophet to their advantage. (The gods of the likes of Pashur, whatever their official garbs or liturgies or protestations, are recognizably—other.)

Priest Pashur is above all prudent, and reasons thus: after all (Who can rightly say?), this Jeremiah may be in touch with some form of "higher power"; and the times are chancy; a barbarian is at the gates; let us then see: it may be that the "Whoever" of Jeremiah, fittingly invoked, will come to our aid, help us turn a dangerous corner.

Magic? Yahweh a mere "deus ex machina"? One senses the anger, the insult to Jeremiah.

His response is a catalog of disaster, far more than bargained for—a bolt of lighting, devastating. Not only does Jeremiah signal an absolute rejection of the fatuous proffer, the attempt to induct Yahweh into the temple pantheon. Specific, terribly detailed is the riposte.

King and priest and people are shortly to perish. Worldly violence along with worldly religion are doomed.

21:11–22:19. A somewhat repetitious stipulation. Jeremiah is forthwith formally dispatched—to the "king, officials, and the people of Jerusalem." The well-being and continuity of the dynasty depend on the keeping of covenant. "Do what is just and right!" We are on familiar prophetic territory, a morality grounded in simple duty toward the innocent and defenseless: "Aliens, orphans, widows," and especially children, victims of obscene sacrifice. Each of these innocents stands at the heart of covenant (Exod. 22:20–26; Lev. 19:33–34; Deut. 10:18–19; 24:17). Their fate is the measure of all else—of the quality of worship or honor accorded Yahweh.

In the world's estimate, the measure may be judged inconsiderable.

No matter the world's "morality." In Yahweh's eyes, those at the foot of the social scale are of serious, even decisive, import. Look ye to this. How constant the reminder: almost as though every generation were belaboring its own memory, in a guileful, intense effort—to suppress its common inheritance, tradition, experience, conscience.

Who will rid us of these meddlesome Jeremiahs? How shall we shuck off the reproof they level at us, pointing, accusing, denouncing, turning our unwilling eyes to the deprivation and misery of the forgotten ones in our midst? All honor to numbing of spirit, to selfishness and greed! These are the secular spur.

And we are drawn out of the inhuman or subhuman pit, barely, by the few who hold firmly in hand a lifeline; who mercifully cast it in our direction; who remind us of our mindlessness; who in season and out summon us to awaken; who raise from the dead our battered humanity.

The passage is nothing if not clear: a "way" to be followed, or not; an either-or of behavior and consequence. And how vividly put, with what plangent tenderness! "To Me, Judah's royal palace is beautiful as the slopes of Lebanon...."

No soft or easy love here, but outrage at the spectacle of love despised. An eye, lucid as a burning glass, is focused on those who refuse healing: the unjust, the raptors of covenant. "You have worshiped and served other gods."

The names of those dark eminences? Mammon and Mars.

22:13–19 Commoner, king, no matter:
cursed be you, whose dwelling's
foundation is injustice,
whose surfeit is cheat,
whose neighbors languish
in chill penury.

    And you
laved in luxury,
make sport of rectitude.
Your house I condemn—
a house of Atreus,
a cenotaph, you
self-condemned
to the second death.

No mourning for you—
like a dead beast dragged
horn, hoof
off and away—
out of sight, of mind
to charnel house,
to hacker's knife!

22:24–27. Something new and startling appears on the human scene, an epiphany. Thus Yahweh decrees through Jeremiah: there shall be one and the same morality for all. The circle is closed; let no one, however exalted, place himself outside the ring of accountability.

O would that!

And what an image is summoned—the signet ring, more than decor, a symbol of authority carefully guarded, crucial for authenticating official documents. Then this awesome image: though the king were God's own signet "on My right hand," yet would he be "pulled off" God's finger.

And "cast afar"—Babylon again.

22:28–30. It is as though the exile were an accomplished fact. (Which it is, and this before the Jerusalemites are rounded up and herded outward.)

The king is a broken jar, a heap of useless shards. In a sense noted before, the exile comes as an anticlimax; prior to the catastrophe, king and people are exiled from their true selves, captors of, captive to— no-covenant.

A New Heart in Evil Times (23:1–24:10)

23:1–6. Two eras are closely contrasted. There are the evil days, the present, rife with deceit and treachery. The leaders are chiefly to blame. They offer nothing; one thinks of "the center" the poet Yeats speaks of that "cannot hold."

King follows king, from bad to worse, as though by a malign law of nature. One ruler, evil or stupid or violent as the case may be, breeds another more evil. The leaders, in Bonhoeffer's phrase, have become the misleaders. In consequence the people are scattered, confused in mind, victimized by false promises, by bread and circuses. The led have become the misled.

We learn as we ponder the times of Jeremiah (and our own!) that little relief arrives "from within." The situation is circular, and closed. The society is ill; its illness is—itself, imminent, genetic. Ill, at once victimizer and victim, it cannot be thought capable of bringing healing to pass. The analysis, woeful as it is, is a unique biblical gift. In comparison, social critics (let alone politicians or conventional religionists) are of little avail.

Those who think to apply conventional remedies serve only to multiply moral and political confusion. Wearyingly, they advocate various nostrums, verbal drugs, promises of relief, formulas of salvation, self-justifying "excusing causes," invocations of the favored god of the moment, pointing of fingers at enemies or hostile neighbors or— much-favored victims at the dark moment—immigrants or the poor in our midst.

No such nonsense from Jeremiah.

Something utterly different: the diagnosis of a skilled surgeon of the spirit, "touching the joining place of flesh and spirit," naming the situation aright—sin and high crime. (And we have seen the cost implicit in such courage; the "patient" has no stomach for the truth.)

Verses 3 and 4 give a word of comfort, nonetheless. Jeremiah, we come also to understand, is free of the tyranny of mere time as it ticks away, a mechanism of gloom and doom. He reads time differently than either executioner or victim. For he admits to neither part.

His century wears the guise of an artful dodger, huckster, hustler. Political and military "experts" push their wares: violence, domination, prospering of a few, misery for multitudes. And the people, stuck fast in falsehoods, are urged to forget the promise.

And yet two events will show forth the truth of the promise. The first (vv. 3 and 4) is the ingathering of the people, scattered, demoralized, in exile. And of no less import, the promised "return" is a psychological metaphor.

Like a Lear on the heath raving, long gone in madness, the culture will recover its sanity. Love, to risk a cliché, will bring it to its senses. It (we) will regain the lost art of judgment, repentance, a sense of creaturehood, of boundaries, of obedience to covenant.

The gist of verses 5 and 6: Look to it, people. The second event is announced in a freshet of poetry. In the "days" that "are coming" shall occur the springing (a "second spring" indeed) of Messiah, the "branch of David." His name Jeremiah has by heart: "Yahweh our Justice," or "our Salvation," or "our Righteousness."

Others than Jeremiah rejoiced in the One who is to come: Isaiah (9:5, 6; 11:1–9), Zechariah (3:8; 6:12), Micah (5:1–5), Amos (9:11), Hosea (3:5).

23:5–6 A DAY IS TO COME,

> I swear it—
> a great day—
>   One
>   nears—
> at hand, right hand.
> No longing, peering the horizon—
>   no more "shall come."
>
> Look for the day, the dawn—
> righteousness the orb,
>   wisdom the scepter.
>
> Behold he comes quickly.
>   Come, Lord Jesus.

Indeed we must speak of the hope here celebrated as a substantial of prophecy itself. It is a literal hope against hope, promulgated as it is in the teeth of the worst times, proceeding as it does from pure faith: a faith that both impels and rewards covenantal fidelity.

Further, a faith that implies a great refusal. With a sense of lively contempt, a faithful people shucks off a victim role—mute, passive, resigned, otherworldly—a role urged, even imposed, by the overriding culture (including abusive religion).

Jeremiah knows it: the One who is to come is already present and accounted for. The Messiah is a social and personal reality, both.

The Savior is—ourselves, united with the Immanuel of Isaiah who beckons, leading us on; the God-with-us, the One who, here and now, walks beside those who walk out of slavery, toward the promise.

If liberation theology (surely a tautology of note) means anything, it means something like the above. Rejected out of hand is the "here and now" arrangement, a social tyranny constructed with malice aforethought, an impasse, abusive and enslaving.

The "here and now" of the Messiah is understood as totally other than this: no dead-end, no detours, no enslavers and slaves! Here and now, the great hinge of the door of a tomb swings wide. Signed and sealed over and captive to death as we have been—nonetheless a perennial dream at length comes true.

Christians know it, are called to know it, to celebrate it, to walk in its light—to admit no impediment. Down dog death!

An event impossible to human endeavor, to the leap of genius, has come to pass. Someone is, after all, risen. Death has lost its claw and fang. On the tongue of the new creation is a new word—Alleluia.

23:9–22 HEARTBROKEN I STAND—

Your word,
a vagrant bird, southward
speeding from world's winter,
has fled my lips.

That wine, that word
bloodies my life, stains
like a lamb's life
lintel and doorpost, Xs me—
Yours.

What make I
  (what make You)
of those others, blathering
fair words in foul weather,
peace for conflict, high noon
for night's blear?

  Who sent them, whose
    credential?

  Never mine—
to set minds awry, the time's
intent
  bent like a bow
strung and sprung
  straight to self-advantage.
My people they urge
  astray, to dead-ends,
  to abattoir, to death of soul.

  Of Sodom, Gomorrah
  (never Jerusalem the holy)—
  their reeking tongues, their
    gross and
    native ground.

In our world, the truth seldom goes uncontested. We have seen it before. Let a Jeremiah appear; on the moment there springs up a coven of opposition, peddling other versions of God, of community, of moral behavior. The Jeremiahs are rare, that strong unmistakable presence, a veritable field of force. Then the opposition proliferates and bears down implacable, over and against the truth-teller.

Still, in the ensuing conflict, the advantage is not altogether to the lackey "court prophets." The truth-teller, we note, knows falsity thoroughly and well, diagnoses and probes the soul of the opponent.

But the entrepreneurs of lies and party lines and winds of chance— these know nothing of truth, and perhaps less of the truth-teller.

The hatred mounts and mounts. The word of God shakes the thrones, calls royal behavior in question, invokes judgment. No one, however exalted, is spared. The opponents are prophets and priests; they are also officers in the king's palace.

Persecution, one thinks, is inevitable.

The enemies make common cause; hatred of the prophet is a close adhesive. More: the court claque senses that winds of chance may be blowing in their favor. Calamity is at the gates, and the official intercessors know nothing of it, or pretend to know nothing. Their words remain placating, reassuring.

Such gods as they pay tribute to bless the evil times, and call them good. "They say to those who despise Me, 'Yahweh has said, "You will have peace"'; and to those who walk in the stubbornness of their heart, they say, 'Disaster will not come to you.'"

These are forms of practical idolatry, though they commonly go under more acceptable names. Jeremiah tells it: one coterie "spoke in the name of Baal and led My people astray." The "Baals" are the "princelings of this world" whom Paul will name and indict as "principalities and powers."

They are ultimately the forms of the spirit of death at large in the world, signs and presences of the Fall, hidden persuaders, beckoners of the mighty, urging them to further unconscionable folly.

In our day the same powers legitimate the "law of the land," act as guardian spirits of "justice systems" and world banks and prisons and abortion clinics and torture chambers and death rows. They normalize the excesses of the Pentagon, the military budget, the "necessary military intervention." They are charged with the smooth functioning of the systems of the Fall.

And well concealed as to intent and aim, they function outside moral scrutiny or accountability. Untouchable, dovetailed one to another in self-interest and mutually assured guilt, they shore up a system of misery and exploitation. They judge and condemn others, especially the prophets and saints—and they are never judged. Or so it seems.

Long after the murderous fact, a curious episode was revealed concerning the elite Acatyl Battalion of the Salvadoran military. On a certain night, their leaders resolved on the murder of the Jesuits at the University. Before departing on their errand, the officers ended deliberations with a prayer in common, for the "success of their mission."

23:23–32. Of dreams and their inconsequentiality. We have a strong indication of the biblical bias against magic, considered commonly as the recourse and refuge of "dwellers on earth."

Today one thinks, in this regard, of the universal, absolute reliance on technique, to set awry things right. Wendell Berry writes of this:

Always, the assumption is that we can first set demons at large and then, somehow, become smart enough to control them. This is not childishness. It is not even "human weakness." It is a kind of idiocy, but perhaps we will not cope with it and save ourselves until we regain the sense to call it evil.

The trouble is, as in our conscious moments we all know, that we are terrifyingly ignorant. The most learned of us are ignorant. The acquisition of knowledge always involves the revelation of ignorance—almost is the revelation of ignorance. Our knowledge of the world instructs us first of all that the world is greater than our knowledge of it. (Wendell Berry, *Standing by Words* [Berkeley, Calif.: North Point Press, 1983])

In contrast to the technicians are the Jeremiahs, mindful, vigiling, alert, great hearkeners of the word, aware of realities hidden from dreamers captivated by the supposed power and beneficence of technique.

23:33–40. The exegetes are unhelpful here. By that I mean—it is one matter to describe a passage as "late" or "very complicated." And quite another to reject it as a text "that really says nothing" (Rudolph). Dare one venture that, now and then, the eye of the expert fails, misses a hidden, nonetheless crucial, message?

The key word, played upon at some length, is "oracle." (The length of the passage slows the mind, gives us pause; Jeremiah is perhaps underscoring something of importance.) The oracle in fact implies the raising of several questions regarding prophecy in general. Who is the author of a given oracle, who stands by it, owns it, testifies to its truth?

There is heavy conflict here. Jeremiah claims the oracles, testifies to their divine origin, therefore to their truthfulness. But his claim runs counter, undergoes a fierce challenge; an opposing coterie has other, very different, "oracles" to offer. His are crusty, morbid at times, curmudgeonly. Theirs are uplifting, irenic, heartening, serendipitous. More, they enjoy fervent support, visible and audible to all, in altitudinous places.

He stands all but alone, he and his Yahweh.

Who then is to be believed? The question, one ventures, has been long since answered. The court prophets peddled their version of events, issuing to kings and people words calculated to fend off trouble, to please and reassure and preserve an odious system (at least for a time) intact.

Time passed, the tactic proved faulty. The text developed, was passed on, eventually reached our eyes. And the terms of their conflict with Jeremiah were clarified.

Events caught up with them, gave them the lie, these not-so-hidden persuaders, along with the eminences they spoke for. Catastrophe befell the system; the web of law and order fell to rot, dissolved. The enemy descended from the north, and prevailed; the populace was decimated, driven into exile.

So in time, the highly placed adversaries were reduced to a subtext, their place in history to a secondary one, if that. They survived as a kind of foil, setting off the brilliant jewel of Jeremiah's truth.

24:1–10. The passage neatly concludes a condemnation that began in 21:1–10.

Amos too had a vision of "ripe fruit" (8:1–3). Both passages show a similar structure. First comes the visionary symbol; then Yahweh questions the prophet as to its meaning.

As to time and place, the Jeremian scene is dolorous in the extreme. All is lost: the terrible exile is a matter of record. The leaders are dead or vanished; so presumably are their tintinabulous prophets. The "temple of the Lord" before which the baskets of fruit are placed, is void.

For years and years, rotten fruits were offered there; the basket aptly signifies fealties accorded the Baals. Rotten liturgies were nicely dovetailed with social and personal misconduct, with injustice and greed and violence.

At verse 6, at long, wearying last, the second phase of Jeremiah's vocation is underway; now he is told to "build and not overthrow, plant and not uproot." There is irony aplenty here; a mingling of the intent of Yahweh and Jeremiah. One imagines the prophet breathing deep, relieved.

The "no" that echoed hauntingly throughout the preceding oracles, a sentence of doom against the powers, is at one stroke vindicated. And lifted.

The newborn "yes" takes flight from his heart, a breath of spring, a flock of released swallows. And yet one insists (Jeremiah insists) that the beauty of the new phase, the approval of human life implied, nonetheless depended on the prior, costly "no." He dragged that daunting monosyllable across the page for years, like a beast of burden bound to a plowshare.

How straitly he was bound to it, to utter, repeat, underscore—and suffer the consequence.

We remember, and are chastened.

So hateful, yes so dangerous to the powerful and their papmongers was that "no" of Jeremiah, as to provoke a death sentence against the naysayer.

Verbum sapientibus satis!

The verse 7: "I will give them a new heart, with which to understand that I am the Lord." There are many, a myriad, ways of stating the promise—as many as there are images of creation. Here we have one of the most ardent, a warmhearted, all-but-physical embracing of the human.

A new heart—Who has not longed for it, knowing all too well the cold, slow beat, the insufficiency, caprice, and selfishness of the old? And who, at the same time, has not felt the spirit shriveling within, how the "old" cannot fire the soul, how convention and habit and rote and moral boredom seize on and throttle other images—those of clairvoyance, of a frenzied sense of justice, of hope itself?

One thing is clear (at least to Yahweh, if not to us): along with the ferocious plundering of the resources of the planet, our spiritual resources also dwindle, all but vanish. Eventually we cannot imagine ourselves as a new people, noncompetitive, compassionate, nonviolent.

We stand benighted amid the ruin of creation, our little triumphs offering what squalid comfort they may: technique and its violence, an economy in shambles, public and private misery festering. A stalemate, the end of a road that went wrong—When, how long since?

The word of Yahweh is clear. The One who knows the heart, who sets it beating, weak or heroic, must act, intervene.

"They shall return to Me with their whole heart."

Only look and see! The text speaks of a change of heart, irrevocably promised. It is to come, says Yahweh. Hearts will be humanized, social structures will follow suit. If within you a new heart, then around you as well—the heart of one beating to the rhythm of all!

It is here, it has come, declares a later and greater prophet: "The Realm of God is ['exists' underscored, here and now] within you."

Interminably, questions arise in this matter of the promise.

Mostly the questions are posed by serious but confounded people. Disheartened by evidence of a social fabric far gone in rot, they come to regard the promise as a failed dream. Its "coming" is contradicted by a hundred experiences, plain to the eyes, painful in the extreme. Wherever one turns, for relief, for hope, a like dolorous sight; every area of life malfunctioning, falling short, falling to pieces.

Families at odds, the church fatuous and sexually obsessed, a rapacious economy, bellicose foreign policies, a mad arms race. And a political spectacle worthy of ancient, decaying Roman imperialists—squads of politicos, boring, incompetent, mean-spirited, morally dilapidated, uncouth of speech, vying with one another for pride of place, for lucre.

Where then has fled that famous promise of God? In what is one to believe, to whom entrust the future, the children?

We come to believe by doing. Or better, in accord with our text, by responding. The initiative of God ("I will give them a heart to understand") is demonstrated whenever one concludes (along with others similarly alert) that the promise, the Messiah, the Coming, the Realm—these are matters requiring close attention and labor. Matters whose outcome rests in our hands also, our proper concern, our vocation in sum.

So realizing, we live on that basis—living and laboring as though the word were true, as though we were called to help it come true, however clumsily or untidily or partially.

These "people of the Realm" live and work and cherish one another and serve the victims and scrutinize closely the law (and at times violate its stupid inequities) on all sides. For whom, ample thanks to our God! Spontaneously it would seem, impelled by a commonly held revulsion against the "system," they gather in communities.

Their common life, varied as to talent and calling, is recognizably similar. They keep goods in common, share household and other tasks across gender lines. They honor a religious tradition with prayer and ritual. They serve the poor of their area; some among them depart to serve in troubled areas elsewhere.

In public they regularly cross lines and barriers of "law and order," to demonstrate their aversion, their "no" (which they take to be an essential of faith itself), in face of a culture of nukes, smart bombs, junk sales of arms, NAFTAs, and other ill-assorted necrophilic phenomena.

No court prophets here!

Redundant to note (we note it anyway, a small tribute in a great matter) that such communities are hardly attentive, let alone addicted to, the siren chorus of church and state, assuring that (though the times are a bleak midnight of despair and disarray) all goes reasonably well in America.

At times, such Christians tell stories of the momentous sea changes that have overtaken them. Often, it seems, their past is marked by disappointment, even by shame, anger, dashed hope. Someone has failed to come through. A marriage has dissolved under the weight of diverse choices. Or perhaps (a great blessing), one's education, linked in the mind of parents and friends to expectation of a payoff, has proven vain. And the scales fell from the eyes. And tears as well.

By force of such happenings, one is granted in due time to utter the "no" of Jeremiah, against a culture whose close metaphors are a bear pit, a swamp of betrayal, greed, and violence. And one is granted a benefit and blessing: entrance into a mature community with an honorable work, freely undertaken. A vocation in short.

Perhaps the story of another is of the church, its authority and teaching. Disappointment again, and even rage: a church that shows its hand, gloved with mail, a church unable or unwilling (or both, often it comes to the same thing) to welcome human diversity.

Something or other stuck like a plank in the eye of the beholding authorities—something irritating, an impurity or incompleteness. One is a woman, or gay—or bears some other default in nature. Due to it, one is to be stigmatized, morally impugned, or put bodily to the door, an outsider, unwelcome, unshriven. Thus the morality of the neo-perfectionists, the latter-day Pharisees.

Whether such memsahibs will long serve to obscure the gentleness and compassion of Christ remains to be seen. Meantime and all unwitting, through sexual and gender bigotry, and no less noxious welcoming of big money and corrupt politicians and absurd religious spectacles, such eminences perform a service of note. They hasten the end of the night they have summoned.

Sub specie aeternitatis (even *temporis*), such events as we endure in a benighted time are of merely hypothetical interest. No doubt the Fall has reasserted its lethal power of darkening minds and hearts.

But keepers of the promise are by no means allowed to give up. They are called to be all the more intent on responding to the word of God, in all its urgency: to assemble, keep vigilant, fast and pray, persevere in love for one another.

The night of the long knives is indeed upon us. But the night and the knives are hardly the entire story. Our days, our awful years, are also a prelude, fast arriving, indeed already quietly, humbly present, of the time "to build...and to plant,'" the time of the Dayspring from on high, of the Coming, the Messiah, of "My day."

Wherefore a muted Alleluia.

10
Baruch, Faithful and Skilled, Keeps True Record
(25:1–29:32)

Twenty-Three Years of Truth-Telling: Nothing Accomplished (25:1–13)

We are offered a summation. Twenty-three years Jeremiah has de-voted to his vertiginous calling. And for all that, the heartache and tears, the words spoken and disregarded and spoken again—still the "system" remains intact. It has its own means and momentum, and stands. To all seeming it yields to no contrary force, human or divine.

More than two decades of this laborious love. To all appearances, our prophet is spectacular only in this: the clamorous unanimity of his rejection.

We pause over the text, taking note of current transpirings. With the toppling of the Berlin Wall and similar events, the "evil empire," we are told, has been surpassed—by all accounts vanquished by the "virtuous," ourselves.

But the happy event, much celebrated in political prattle, has brought no relief from the bellicose behavior of the virtuous victors. Those forces formerly intent on (not to say obsessed by) the delicious prospect of the enemy's destruction have hardly become thoughtful or changed direction.

The nuclear arms race proceeds at full speed, unimpeded, though due to the iniquity of what enemy, new or old, one is hard put to say. And a further development: our "virtuous" conduct in the world has been domesticated, turned inward. We are now intent on virtuously disposing of, demonizing, victimizing, causing to disappear from public places, those multitudes whom the system itself has created—which is to say, the unproductive poor.

A species of ethnic cleansing is underway in the cities; it is marked by an unexampled ferocity. A common understanding, unimpeded by a contesting sense of the human, is darkly at work. It implies a bold, momentous shift away from biblical anthropology, as this is exemplified in the lives and counsels of the prophets.

Let church, synagogue, mosque, take notice. The culture is hell bent on creating its own version of the (sic) "human."

What is that version to look like? We are scarcely left in the dark, offered as we are, so to speak, prototypes, day after day. One such: in a carefully orchestrated salvo of the media, a chief tactician of the Gulf slaughter was touted as a presidential candidate. He prudently withdrew from the race. But in or out, it remains striking that the question of his accountability for war crimes was not once raised. Nor will it be.

Meantime, in center ring of the national circus, a clamorous nonentity rules the Congress. To all but universal silence—or in many places to acclaim—he plies the whip freely, leading a crusade of political pimps against the poor.

The White House is mesmerized by the spectacle. Its inhabitants, it would seem, have at command neither moral conviction nor even an enlightened expediency, wherewith to counter the plague of the demagogue, denounce him—or raise a plea for the voiceless.

Thus is suggested a contemporary version of the twenty-three years of Jeremiah. His voice, as he grimly reports, is quite lost on the winds. What a summary, offered by so great a soul; and what desolation rises from the page!

We too have had our prophets, more or less unheeded in the long or short run. Gandhi, Merton, Dr. King, Dorothy Day, and César Chávez; the martyrs of Salvador, Guatemala, Nicaragua, South Africa, Eastern Europe, East Timor, Indonesia, and Burma—a myriad of Jeremiahs, unable, for all the heroism of their lives and deaths, to stem the torrent of a universal Babel, its confusion and omniviolence.

If that were all, if such lives had attained only the honor of heroic death, if our belabored history could be brought up short by the swords of murderous opportunists—we were indeed lost. But that is not the whole story. We rejoice, we celebrate, we take heart from—the something more.

Which brings us back to Jeremiah and his years of shouting into the winds.

Was ever a human more entitled to roll up the scroll once for all and shrug and make his way homeward? "I gave them my best, and nothing came of it.... Leave them then, to their own ruin." He never spoke it, such an antitext.

And because he did not turn back or give up in the cruelly unequal fray, something momentous, something to our point also—something to the point of hope—follows.

Twenty-three years gone. And the task never finished with. He would perhaps say: not even begun.

And yet, and yet.

This: the adamantine opposition, ill serving as it seemed, in reality served him well. Day by day, year by year, by little and by little, his vocation was clarified.

At this or that point of personal crisis, he took heart once more, determined to go on, however obscure the road. That was the saving element, the grace, bare and to the bone. He would not be silenced. Had not Yahweh conferred on him "a heart with which to understand"?

Of this pertinacity, this valiant will, something was born (though he would never see it born). Across the centuries, Jeremian communities arose. In light of their perdurance against the worst odds, even in our benighted day, the twenty-three years of our prophet are hardly to be thought fruitless. The discouragement and sense of futility were—premature; the short run yielded to the long.

Must one invoke the old Roman poet, Horace? Montes parturient, nascetur ridiculus mus? (Years and years of labor—and nothing gained?). To the contrary. The book of Jeremiah rests in our hands—after some twenty-six centuries! Still viable, still our handbook, beloved, telling, filled with thundering intuitions, intensely human.

So alive, so near. It is as though the prophet held the scroll before our eyes, as though his eyes met ours over the text. As though he cries aloud: keep on keeping on!

A personal word may befit here. My friends and I count more "years of no outcome" than those totted up by Jeremiah. From 1968 and the burning of the files at Catonsville to the present writing in 1996/97, we count innumerable arrests, trials, jailings of ourselves and our friends across the land. No one, or very few, have given up. The communities from time to time waver and grow wan, but gather steam again, are for the most part intact.

What of our spirits? Wildly veering at times—jeremiads of our own composing loud on the air go unheeded (as per our original saint, recorded with such pain!), altogether unheeded by the entrenched powers, judges, police, presidents, Pentagon, and their servile media.

1968–1996. More years than Jeremiah's, more symbolic actions, a non-outcome strangely parallel to his. Or to put matters more exactly—a worse public situation than when we began. Deranged politically, economically ruinous. More terrible weaponry, more of creation laid waste, more misery in the streets.

Every excuse, in sum, for giving up the game with a parting jeremiad: "I spoke untiringly, but you would not listen.... "

On the fiftieth anniversary of Hiroshima in August of 1996, hundreds were arrested across the land at those unblinking, sleepless Cerebri of empire: the Pentagon, the nuclear think tanks, the military installations of every mad hue. As Einstein wrote, the Bomb changed everything except the hearts of its creator-creatures.

To those with an eye half open, the intervening years offer a glimpse, sobering and plenary, of the adamantine heart of darkness.

And yet, and yet, the communities do not give up; in our estimate, that matter of no outcome is of secondary import. We offer no excuse for deflection or dereliction. As in the encounters of Jeremiah with the principalities, their obduracy serves a purpose contrary to its intent: it strengthens and reawakens.

"That which does not kill me, only makes me stronger" (Ho Chi Minh).

And the promise held out to Jeremiah in his youth is also ours for the asking; strength meeting strength. "Be not crushed on their account, as though I would abandon you. It is I this day who have made you a fortified city, a pillar of iron, a wall of brass, against the whole land."

Yet another subtle lesson lurks within the present text, with its interplay of threat and promise. This: if hearts come round to the godly way, the outcome is one of perennial "at-home-ness": "You shall remain in the land which Yahweh gave you and your ancestors, forever."

If not, if a befouled fealty to the Baals continues, "this whole land will be a ruin and a desert; for seventy years these nations shall be enslaved to the king of Babylon." Exile, from holiness, from our own humanity, is the penalty of infidelity.

The facts of the case surrounding Jeremiah provide a telling metaphor. There was, we learn, no repentance; and the exile of an entire people shortly followed.

But perhaps it bears repeating: psychologically, spiritually, a form of exile was underway long before the Babylonians "came down like a wolf on the fold." And Jeremiah was the first to suffer the consequence of this alienation, in public contempt and violence against his person.

These he bore, as he is at pains to inform us, for many (fruitless) years; but the canker, a disease in the bloodline, festered long before. And it outlasted his life.

During those years of unmitigated obduracy, the kings and the people looked past him or through him. It was as though he hardly existed, except as an impediment to their rakes' progress; to be gotten around, to be trodden on. They were spiritually displaced, deranged, at sea, blind to the gift, the moral greatness and goodness that stood before them. So they lived and died apart from the root and center and source of existence, "following," as they did, "strange gods."

Thus the first meaning of the exile is not a geographic uprooting at all, as Jeremiah implies (and our own experience and modern psychology testify). Our lifetime furnishes numerous heroic accounts of survival under atrocious conditions—the death camps, eviction and exile, torture chambers, gulags; Auschwitz to Long Kesh to the Tiger Cages of Vietnam to the Bunderstaands of South Africa. Under such conditions, coping and surviving, many among the persecuted learn the bitter ways of hope against hope, the discipline of Bible study and prayer.

Most die; many die well; some few survive to recount in tones of level calm, the lacerations of body and spirit—and the altogether unlikely coming through.

Biblical exile also implies covenant, whether observed or violated. The truly human, we are reminded, demands—connection. To God, to the neighbor. Thus Jeremiah and the other giants insist in season and out; integral worship implies justice, peaceableness, and compassion in daily behavior.

Bowing before the Baals, on the other hand, implies loss of the true way, of the Soul of our souls, the Heart of our hearts. And inevitably, loss of the sense of one another; domestic injustice and greed; and abroad, arms and war.

All this Jeremiah saw and mourned and raged against. So mysterious—the "lost" years of our beloved prophet undergo a sea change; they take the form of an ironic victory.

Did he come to understand? Nothing was lost. What nobler life than one passed in heroic vindication of truth! Could we too but believe it!

Be comforted, Jeremiah. Then and now, servitude to idols is the only loss.

At 25:10, we come once more to the intriguing question: Is it Yahweh or Jeremiah who speaks? Perhaps both in chorus, two hearts as one, hearts that for the space of a lifetime have beat in close unison.

And here, as in the book of Revelation, lies a harmony of grief so subtle, measured, true. Indeed the prophet, and prophetic Yahweh, know this; for all its moral ugliness, imperial culture is capable of triumphs of the spirit, of ecstatic peaks, great art, music, architecture. Like Paul, we too rejoice in "all that is true, all that is good."

And then the destruction of all, the deaths, the exile. Surely mourning befits too, for all that beauty, lost, forfeited, wasted. Amid the triumphs of high culture, simple things pass away, will be no more: "the song of joy and the song of gladness, the voice of the bridegroom and the voice of the bride, the sound of the millstone and the light of the lamp."

All stopped short, all quenched.

As in Revelation (18:24), the "strong angel" takes up the threnody all but word for word. Yet another empire collapses, and "the sound of millstone will not be heard in thee any more. And light of lamp will not shine in thee any more. And voice of bridegroom and of bride will not be heard in thee any more."

The Chosen Fall First (25:15–38)

Now the cup of God's wrath is held out to the nations. The hand that extends the cup is Jeremiah's.

We have an ironic turn about of the universality of Isaiah (chap. 2 and passim). Here, the nations are summoned to judgment; but no promise is held out, whether of salvation or mercy. "They shall drink and stagger and go mad" (25:16).

More, and worse: Jeremiah offers a prelude to Paul's vision of the empires, who but for the mercy of God are no more than a *massa damnata*. "For there is no distinction, all have sinned and have need of the glory of God" (Rom. 2:23).

The theme closes in; it is suffocating, this version of God's scrutiny upon the world. According to Jeremiah, judgment is inevitable—indeed it is already underway. In this fashion: the most belligerent, secular, materialistic among the empires, those which lord it over creation, take slaves, win wars, lay hand on world markets, in every conceivable sense play God—these are summoned for judgment (here, and in more detail in chaps. 46–51).

The enumeration of those hailed before the court is distressingly complete. No exemption, no "holy nations." Summoned first of all in the litany of accountability is—"Jerusalem! Then the cities of Judah, her kings and princes, to make them a ruin and a desert, an object of ridicule and cursing, as they are today" (25:18). The religious entities to come forward first? Those whose status has led them perennially to seek exemption, to explain away their delicts, to excuse themselves and invoke, with all piety, God's choice? How comes it that such as these are found in first place on the implacable list of the accused, the presumed guilty?

Experts remind us that the crucial verse 18 is by way of a gloss. Ironically, Jerusalem and the cities of Judah were summoned later. But some clairvoyant scribe pushed them forward, an eminence of shame. Still, a question remains: Does the late inclusion weaken the argument? Or might it be thought a necessary correction of the earlier text?

In any case, taking our version as it stands, it seems that in the eyes of Yahweh the behavior of the people of covenant differs in no substantial way from that of the despised "dwellers on earth." The scroll of the law is closed against the light. Injustice, fraud, greed, war-making pollute the air. The appalling tegument of crime covers the earth; the shroud is woven close.

And: Come to judgment, Jerusalem first of all!

The "cup of judgment" is a familiar image (49:12; Hab. 2:15, 16; Ezek. 23:32–34; Isa. 51:17–23; Lam. 4:21; Pss. 60:5; 75:9). Here, the cup is joined to another highly charged, ambiguous offering: "The sword I shall send among them."

The cup contains a dangerous mix indeed: "They shall drink and stagger and go mad." And later, the awful instruction proceeds, the potion proves lethal: "Drink, become drunk and vomit, fall and rise no more" (v. 27).

It seems that the drama of the cup and that of the sword are one. Drinking from the cup, the nations dramatize their shameful behavior. In the understanding of Yahweh and Jeremiah, they are habitually drunk; murder, injustice, greed, maltreatment of the innocent—these bespeak no sanity, but minds ghoulish, inflamed, grisly, plain mad.

The cup brings matters to a head, while the sword cuts deep: "I will call down the sword upon all the dwellers upon earth" (a euphemism for the criminal empires). And the insistence: judgment falls first upon the chosen.

An ironic note: understandably, the nations are reluctant to drink from the lethal cup. But Yahweh's instruction to Jeremiah, his cup-bearer, is implacable: "If they refuse to take the cup from your hand and drink, say to them: Thus says the Lord of hosts: You must drink! For since I begin to inflict evil upon this city which is called by My Name, how can you possibly be spared?" (25:28–29).

In the eyes of Yahweh, the argument a fortiori is irrevocable, irrefutable. If I do not spare My once-chosen, how will it go with you, who know Me not?

Nonaccountability is the veritable law of the nations, the only "international law" they bow to. Lawlessness is their law; bowing out, buying out, bailing out—these are the secular liturgies of the empires. Prophecy is the swift correction of this, its rebuke, the text that pre-empts and cancels the inflation and pretension of the congresses of superhumans.

We ponder chapter 25, and we too are discomfited, shaken. The gods of appeasement, the Baals, at ease among the "dwellers on earth" (at ease also in Zion), are nowhere to be seen.

Instead, a torrent of images of rage and fury, drawn from an ecology gone berserk, from the animal world, from war and warriors: "a roaring from on high"; "a shout like that of vintagers over the grapes" (grapes of wrath to be sure); "calamity…from nation to nation"; "the godless …given to the sword"; "whom the Lord has slain…lying like dung on the field"; "the time for your slaughter has come"; "no flight for the shepherds, no escape for the leaders…"; "the lion leaves his lair…. "

("Humankind cannot bear very much reality, sang the bird" [T. S. Eliot].)

What version of reality, what kind of religion—this shattering of the pillars of existence, this absolutely enraged renunciation and refusal of "things as they are," this peremptory summons issued against the high and mighty?

The images! Here and elsewhere (but here most tellingly), we learn much concerning Yahweh's hatreds and loves, rejections and embraces. We are granted a glimpse of the physiognomy of the God of Jeremiah: the leonine One; the wrathful Cup; the Sword; the stormy One; the One and Only; the jealous One; Yahweh, who in the wrathful voice of Jeremiah unmasks and excises the death lurking at the heart of things.

(But what of us? What of our God? What does our God look like? What does our God forbid? To what does our God summon us?)

And a Death Sentence for the Truthful (26:1–24)

The scribe Baruch, we are informed, was witness to the temple diatribe of Jeremiah (Bar. 7:1–15), and transcribed it. (The story is told in so lively a way as to imply an eyewitness, as well as a skilled eye and hand. It is much in the manner of Mark's all but parallel account [14:55ff.], or the public confrontations in Acts [6:11–14; 21:27–31]).

Verses 2 to 6 comprise Baruch's résumé of the temple discourse earlier recorded. What we are offered is a "passion scene," breathtakingly reminiscent of the encounter of our Savior with the powers. No wonder Jeremiah has been embraced by Christians as a type of Christ!

Time and again, we (and Jeremiah) are cast back and back, into the sorry task of "pulling down" and "rooting up." It is never done with. Here again, the good news must include the bad, must be presented also as a "no"—a crucial prelude to a "yes" of substance.

But perhaps we have, as suggested, not a new diatribe, but a reprise of the earlier tough discourse. Presuming the latter, Baruch the scribe would have us know the details of an outcome not heretofore dwelt on. The prophetic message insists all along that crime and consequence are a single reality; that the "two" are in fact a single hyphenated reality. And the opposite is true as well; virtue has its own (not reward—let our term be neutral for the moment) consequence.

But whether we summon our own experience or the biblical data, it seems true; more often than not the outcome of truth-telling will be—dire. As here. And behind the powers that presume to govern this world, the principalities stand. These animate and urge and seek to justify worldly authority with ultimate credentials. These great inhibitors and interferers, resilient and of iron will and perdurance—and outright moral blindness—offer a clue.

It has always been a puzzle: attempt after attempt in our century to justify the creation and perdurance of certain institutions. One thinks of the Pentagon in this regard, or of the CIA or the FBI. The open eye of a child would judge the institutions as manifestly wicked, dedicated as they are with seemingly endless and persistent ingenuity to works of death.

But not at all! Politicos, generals, and the media present such grotesqueries as totally otherwise, as worthy of respect, beneficent, symbolic of the prospering of a great, good-hearted, law-abiding people. Otherwise decent families traverse the continent to visit the great sprawl of the Pentagon, awesomely permanent, disproportionate, overbearing, ugly beyond bearing. It is as though the pilgrims stood on holy ground, before a revered national shrine. The children are brought along; a guided tour can be arranged.

And among the reassuring wonders, implying the intact estate of national values, a "meditation room" is pointed out. The heart of the Beast is—piety.

Nothing of human malice or blindness serves to explain the existence of such a monstrosity, the prospering of those engaged in its unholy deeds. One is well advised to have recourse to the Bible. There, especially in Paul's letter to the Ephesians, we are reminded of a truth crucial to sanity; the Pentagon bespeaks something surpassing our collective lunacies or world-class belligerence.

The canker is of a different order, as William Stringfellow realized so acutely. "Our wrestling is not against flesh and blood, but against the Principalities and Powers, against the world rulers of this darkness, against the spiritual forces of wickedness on high" (Eph. 6:12).

The principalities imply a spirit of domination and death, the "other side" of visible, tactile, audible reality, of the manifestly prospering, juridically faultless "leaders of the nation." Paul points to the dark side of such institutions: the Pentagon, White House, Supreme Court, "investigative headquarters." Such are evidence in our midst (in our hearts) of the Fall, as that dolorous event touches upon individuals and public life, enticing, persuading, urging the pursuit (as though it were a vocation from God)—of the multiple metaphors of death.

Anyone who has stood at the Pentagon or vigiled there, or poured blood and ashes there (and been arrested there), tends to grow thoughtful, inclines to close heed to the biblical evidence.

The shortcomings of every human explanation become clear in face of the horrid spectacle; each day for some fifty years now, some twenty thousand Americans have entered the vast amphitheater, insufferably ugly, of death-as-social-method.

Theories of socialized inhumanity or collective insanity or collective fear and dread or cold or hot wars go only so far—not far enough by light years. A chief principality is horridly, boldly on display: obscene, unashamed, up front, the cosmic whore of Revelation bedizened with her resources and wares.

"The wiles of the devil," Paul speaks of; then the demonic is further named: "the world rulers of this darkness." World rulers, the ferocious usurpations of empires, from Jeremiah to this day. Then "darkness," bespeaking moral blindness both public and personal. A description, in sum, of the perennial seizure of time and place and institutions and lives and deaths by the Fall.

And further: "the spiritual forces of wickedness on high." Not merely does wickedness take high and mighty form, not only does it aspire through ever more advanced technique, to superhuman status. "On high" is a biblical geography signifying the locale of the divine. The phrase suggests epiphanies, the revelation to us humans, especially to the prophets, of the holy.

Which is to say, the principalities would have us aspire to the status of divinity. They urge the sundering of bonds, of the boundaries of our creaturely estate. "Ye shall be as gods" is their enticement.

Precisely. Let us rise to the status of masters of life and death, of those who (by right, by "divine right") decide who shall live and who die. Such are the magistri of modern war, the godlings with their hands poised above the nuclear triggers.

If the churches on occasion speak of such matters, it is in a muted, undisturbing way. Occasion offering (in the empire, the occasion is frequent; wars proliferate), the "just-war theory," that hoary Trojan horse, is inevitably wheeled out and hauled onstage. The setting is the city (i.e., homeland, markets, gross national income, four freedoms, partners in NATO, SEATO, NAFTA)—beleaguered.

The great equine is wired for sound. Once within the gates it will offer its well-orchestrated "just cause," including of course stipulations of "limitation of casualties," "protection of noncombatants." And shaking its wooden mane in abandon, it will shout learnedly such obfuscations as *ultima ratio.*

No matter the monstrosity is bellyful with the ghosts of special pleaders—shades of warriors, of crusaders and justifiers and popes and theologians. And speaking magisterially for all, as though with final authority, the great shade of Augustine.

No matter there is not the ghost of a Bible to hand.

26:1–19. But to return to our prophet—in 26:1–19, we hear the muffled beat of doom. Deadly charges are leveled against Jeremiah; a death sentence is invoked.

We note the grievous anomaly. The prophet is condemned by religious authorities, the "priests and prophets." And he is rescued from death by secular authorities, the "princes of Judah."

The argument for the defense is of great, though collateral, interest.

The prophet Micah, a contemporary of Isaiah, was likewise "summoned." He prophesied a century before Jeremiah; his images against Judah are uncannily similar to those of the prophet under fire: "Her leaders render judgment for a bribe, her priests give decisions for a salary, her prophets divine for money.... Therefore, because of you, Zion shall be plowed like a field, and Jerusalem reduced to a rubble, and the mount of the temple to a forest ridge" (3:12). Elders intervened; their point proved decisive. Micah also had prophesied doomsday as the awful alternative to repentance. And the people of his era listened, and turned to God.

And what of us?

Jeremiah was released.

(In passing, one notes that the previous prophets were well known in the time of Jeremiah, and their writings were a matter of record, apt for citing.)

Far from suffering the threatened fate of the greater prophet, Micah was granted a serious hearing, and his teachings, stark as they were, influenced the reform of the king, Ezekiah (2 Kings 18:4). (Also, as far as is known, the disaster threatened by Micah was averted [2 Kings 19:35].)

Strange. Here once more, it is the secular authorities who grasp the meaning and intent of sacred history; it is they, not the priests, who come to the defense of Jeremiah by quoting Micah.

It is they who sense how fine and high a wire the prosecution is walking, in threatening a "criminal" proceeding against Jeremiah. "We are on the point of committing a great evil, to our own undoing" (26:19). (Today too we hear of those brought to the bar for the crime of "defaming the state," as in Burma and the former Soviet Union.)

26:20–24. Jeremiah for the moment is spared, if not vindicated, the scribe implies. Indeed a narrow squeak.

The worse fate of yet another prophet, otherwise unknown, is recalled. A certain Uriah, who Baruch hastens to add, also "prophesied in the name of the Lord." His death was sought by the king. Uriah, like

Jeremiah and Micah, had "defamed the motherland." The prophet fled to Egypt. All to no avail. It seems probable that King Jehoiakim, a creature of the Egyptian empire, had an extradition clause written into the treaty of vassalage. According to its terms, political dissidents in flight could be snatched and returned to their homeland for punishment.

The doomed prophet, as Baruch implies strongly (v. 24), had no one to speak for him. He perished, and his teaching is unknown. And what a loss to ourselves, to know so little of so courageous a spirit. Still, one thinks to pause and honor him, a hero of the stature of Jeremiah.

Our prophet is more fortunate by far. Three generations of the same family stand by him (36:25; 39:14; 40:5ff.). In the present crisis, Ahikam of the second generation intercedes, and to good effect.

Baruch the scribe would have us know how close to disaster the contention came—and rejoice.

Armed Resistance? Yahweh Forbids It (27:1–29:32)

A contest against false prophets.

It seems a kind of law of nature. Certainly it is a staple of biblical history; the truth must ever take its stand amid the shadow of falsehood. The shadow, moreover, has a certain substance, sinister and persuasive. More, it has at its side resources of note, highly placed advocates.

Poor truth, poor truth-teller—what a contrast! Jeremiah for his part has hardly any of the above advantages. His word is unrelievedly somber and stark, his "either-or" writ large; undergo conversion of heart, or court catastrophe. Among the powerful he stands alone. The temple prophets wish him ill, and in the court of the king, few if any would plead for him.

Jeremiah *solus*, a spectacle of derision and scorn. At one time he is held in close custody, a prisoner in the stocks. In another episode he is plunged in a filthy well. And in the most serious episode of all, he is brought to trial on a capital charge.

We consider his calling, and we are appalled.

He is to convey the word of Yahweh to a heedless people (as though that were not a sufficient emotional burden!). Meantime he must conduct his life in accord with a code both harsh and arbitrary. At times, the instruction from on high seems gratuitously cruel. He is forbidden marriage and family; his wife dies; he is instructed to forgo all mourning.

He becomes a kind of full-color reflection of whatever divine mood: affection, spleen, tenderness, a choler ferocious and bruising. (His plight reminds one of the fate of the errant bride of Hosea, her meanderings enlarged to a symbol of wayward Israel.) So he too becomes Jeremiah-the-metaphor, his life expanded to (better, reduced to) an image of dire events that are to befall a miscreant people.

No wonder his plight overwhelms; like a Job, he curses the day of his birth.

These crucial chapters, 27–29. As the contest of Isaiah a century earlier, so Jeremiah's. Striking similarities: the theme at issue, the message, the counsel of Yahweh to each, the public word to be conveyed—nonviolence in face of the provocation of war.

This latter is the moral substance of the word of Yahweh to the people, and most strikingly to the kings; and the rub as well.

One could reflect ruefully on the perennial unacceptability of such a word. (And the stricture must include a number of academic commentators, who dwell upon the numerous evidences of a violent Yahweh—and hardly take notice of striking contrary evidence such as this.)

The kings and their coterie of prophets stand pat. Clearly, armed resistance places the lives of the exiles at risk. But the powerful are seldom loath to place others in jeopardy! So it is agreed: an armed face-off with the Babylonian tyrant.

We recall the circumstance of the people around whom the conflict between Jeremiah and the secular officials swirls. The people's situation is humiliating in the extreme. Many are already in exile. To them, too, Jeremiah's message is devastating. The exiles are to submit to their status, vassals of a detested foreigner—and this for an indefinite period. They are to settle in, to intermarry and beget families. And an end of national humiliation is nowhere in sight.

The instruction is stark. More: adding insult to the dark message, Jeremiah delivers it in high dramatic style.

The gathering he enters, probably uninvited, is no ordinary assembly. We have seen the like; it is a staple of secular history.

Those who assemble are power brokers. Their work involves nice adjustments in balances of power, careful measuring of adversaries, weaknesses, and strengths. And a concurrent polity. Common to the players is an assumption of what may be required as a decision of "last resort": whether usurpation, mendacity, coercion, or the threat of armed violence.

The game is hopelessly complex, the talk-talk prolix. And whatever is agreed will fall apart at the next provocation. Here would seem to be the current situation: the small powers adjacent to Babylon seek a military alliance, proposing to include the king of Judah, against the common enemy, Nebuchadnezzar of Babylon. Quite a show they mount (and then they take themselves so seriously!).

King Zedekiah is in a delicate spot. A mere vassal, he rules at the pleasure of a foreign tyrant. And the majority of his influential subjects are already banished. A wrong move would endanger everyone: those who remain in the realm, the foreign exiles, and his own uneasy crown.

The court prophets urge the alliance. They positively exude confidence. The period of exile, they announce, is all but over. More: an armed rebellion against Babylon would be to the advantage of all; among other benefits it would serve to shorten the time of humiliation.

The supposition at work (and of course never mentioned, a matter of noblesse oblige) is plain to Jeremiah. In their own estimate these godlings are pilots of history and prime shapers of creation itself.

They are also dark gamblers. But the stake (who shall live, and who die), momentous as it must be judged, is never once mentioned.

The delegates are, so to speak, great practitioners of practicality. Their deliberations admit of nothing so simpleminded as, say, taking seriously the existence of Yahweh, or determining what his will might be in crucial matters.

Might Yahweh have an opinion concerning the endangerment of the creation, its harrowing in war? Might he not utter, or wish to hear from them, a word of concern for the innocent ones, the noncombatants, the children? Might he not even disapprove of their fervor for war-making?

Very well then, offer them a reminder: God exists; God is hardly banished from the high assembly. Enter Jeremiah.

Weird, shocking. Fool or jester or madman?

His appearance is grotesque—he is bowed under by the yoke of a beast of burden.

Nonetheless, by way of contrast (the ostentatious solemn-faced assembly, the eccentric getup of the mime), the message of Yahweh is powerfully delivered. Its exordium is formal, a proffer of credentials: "It was I who made the earth, and people and beasts on the face of the earth." (Which is to imply: "Who is in charge here?") "...And I give all these to whomsoever I think fit"—a claim, one thinks, designed to counter the machinations of the congress, to reduce, show forth their moral puniness.

If Jeremiah is a shocker, Yahweh is nothing less. There is greater surprise in store. Who is acceptable? Who is to be endowed—and who turned away? Surely it is not they who are rejected, the king, the prophets of a chosen people, their secular cohorts?

Before them all, to their immense discomfiture, Yahweh declares a strange alignment. Yahweh stands with the tyrant: "Now I have given all these lands into the hand of Nebuchadnezzar, king of Babylon, my servant[!]" (27:6).

The purport is plain.

On the one hand, according to every just-war criterion imaginable, those in exile have good cause to rise, cast off their chains, and fight. And yet, and yet. Revolt, armed rebellion, even under harshest of provocation, is here forbidden. The same message: the victims are to submit, to normalize their situation, to assimilate into the odious empire.

And what of those who, for one reason or another, have escaped the fate of the exiles? The Jerusalemites and their ruler receive instructions along similar lines. They are forbidden to urge armed revolt against the tyrant, in support of captive relatives and friends. The prophets among them are to cease and desist their issuing of lucubrations, their hostility toward Jeremiah (vv. 9, 10) and Yahweh.

The orders are issued under threat of direst penalties. The message issued to the delegates is addressed also to King Zedekiah (vv. 12–15) and to priests and people (vv. 17ff.).

This is all quite astonishing. A nonviolent God, amid the multitudinous evidences throughout the Bible of divinely sanctioned violence? In the era of Jeremiah, we take note of this momentous development. Its purport, then or now, is not easily grasped. (Indeed, as noted, it is generally ignored by scholars, theologians, historians.)

Someone has changed, utterly. Who is it—Yahweh or the prophet or the prophet's image of Yahweh? And what are the implications for ourselves?

One has an impression. Perhaps a nonviolent Yahweh has long been peering through the moral fog that envelops humankind. Waiting the moment, the messenger?

Now is the moment, Jeremiah the man. Through him, Yahweh will strive by every wile and stratagem to turn and turn about our ethos of belligerence, our ever-ready provocations, wiles and guiles, demonologies, moral jugglery—to turn these about toward a new moral sense, a new behavior.

Something momentous, something new in the air. We are set off balance. We peer and peer, seeking the physiognomy of Yahweh. He is by no means fully self-revealed, even through so clairvoyant a spirit as Jeremiah.

On the one hand, he abhors and forbids armed conflict. On the other, the summons to nonviolence is couched in the old familiar terms, those of threatened carnage and imminent disaster. Thunderbolts from on high! Obey, or else! Assume a nonviolent stance, or I shall wax—violent!

How we long (or say we long) for instructions free of equivocation, threat, shows of force and domination, in such crucial matters!

And yet, and yet. A greater than Jeremiah has walked our world. And in the matter at hand has issued admirably clear instruction. Has lived in accord with his words, and so died. It would seem, in sum, a matter of Christian faith, that in Christ, the clarity (here purportedly longed for) is at hand. Killing of "enemies," whether sanctioned by the state or not, is forbidden us, once for all.

And the instruction is so clear, detailed, dramatized in his living and dying—as to blind the eye of the believer. All said, we prefer the ancient "shekinah," God in the "cloud of unknowing." How perilous to know too well the divine will, to view too close at hand the behavior of a divine one, under the terrible systems of temple and state!

Blinded we are, and much prefer to be. Perhaps fear, after all, rules the roost—fear of God's way in the world, fear of one another, fear of coming too close, of seeking (and seeing!) the will of God in the nonviolent Christ.

So the Grand Inquisitor, that dark doppelgänger of every believer's fears, was correct. Christian history plainly goes counter to Christ. More, we have declared him—redundant. The proof? The church. The church, with its worldliness and aura of success and grandeur and its wars and usuries and slaveries, celebrates the redundancy of Christ. This is the charge on which the Inquisitor indicts Christ anew, on the steps of a great cathedral: "We need you not. Please to vanish from the earth."

Ours is another errand in time and world than his. Namely: the perennial pursuit of our (undoubtedly Christian, undoubtedly legitimate) interests. Through war—if "necessary," if "just." And note too the circular argument; each of the warring parties may, and does, apply the famous criteria of just war to its own legitimacy. And emerges innocent and justified.

In chapter 28, a contrast: the high priest Hananiah and Jeremiah the nobody; a face-to-face confrontation ensues, vividly recorded, probably by Baruch.

Evidently the high priest has decided on a David-Goliath contest. One against one, and winner take all. The setting is "the house of the Lord."

Before a full assembly, with plenary confidence, Hananiah addresses his adversary. If Jeremiah can quote the word of the "Lord of hosts," so can he. He proceeds to deliver an astonishing message, utterly at variance with that of Jeremiah. To wit: within two years (!) the grip of King Nebuchadnezzar will be broken, and the exiles will be home free.

Two years—or seventy years. Who is to be believed? Jeremiah responds with unexpected complaisance. Unexpected to this extent: in spite of my own assurance of speaking on behalf of Yahweh, how I long that your prophecy prove true!

There is sweetness in his word and bearing, and a deep sense of compassion toward the suffering of the exiles. One cannot but feel for Jeremiah; what a hard yoke he bears (literally as well: that weight of iron on his shoulders).

Still he insists: many before me, Jeremiah, have been messengers of the woe of Yahweh. And more often than not, the doom they announced came to pass. But as to the prophets of peace and plenty and good times to come—these are proven authentic only when their fine words blossom in event. So we must wait and see.

Hananiah too has a sense of drama, and seizes the moment. He takes the yoke bodily from the neck of Jeremiah, breaks it, and says: Thus shall it happen to Babylon. Jeremiah is speechless, bested for the moment. He turns away.

Desolation lies heavy on the page. The old sense of utter futility: once more it washes over him like a filthy tide. Loss of honor and repute, "too long a sacrifice." Years of playing the thankless nemesis, thwarted, persecuted—and to what end?

To this: there arrives yet another skilled tongue, weighted with cunning, adversarial words, quick to wound, plucking the moment of drama, issuing his confident pronunciamento of impending consolation and restoration. (The Jeremian drama plays on. Shall we say, in

Dr. Martin Luther King and Billy Graham, the prophet and the high priest?)

The words of Hananiah are utterly false. And they win hearts and minds, spoken as they are with the insuperable confidence of a mighty counterclaim—that they issue from God. And who is to say him nay?

Jeremiah stops us in our tracks, his unimpeachable integrity. There he stands, shamed and silent. His words and works are stripped naked of advantage, of all impedimenta of prestige and advantage. No burdens of bliss and honor; he bears, like the cross of Christ, the yoke of a slave or animal. He has lost all, save that burdensome yoke of his—the truth.

It was not snatched from him. Under its burden he abides, alone as usual, surrounded with hostility or a baffled bemusement, standing against the tide of political likelihood. And withal, sturdily opposing the alliance. Come what may.

We take note of the tactic of "carrot and stick," the premise of Hananiah, clinching the argument of those urging the alliance. Only two more years of exile, imagine, and all will be well, our loved ones restored to us!

No, not true, insists the stubborn one. God has a longer, harsher sentence of banishment in mind. Like a death knell the word of God. The first generation will die in exile. Two years? Seventy years are decreed. And why, and to what good end?

To bring the people to—teachableness.

Hananiah fascinates: a political strategist of note, his flair for turning the heads of the mobocracy. He has studied well the formulas of prophecy. A very gourmet of language, he chooses his words like a Cassius, ready with unction, seeking above all to please and prevail. He makes great sense, in the way of the world.

Pieties stripped away, the tactic is clear as high noon. He stakes everything on the main chance: the alliance sealed, an uprising, the quick defeat of the tyrant. In sum, we have a moral pigmy, miming, and cleverly, the humiliated, solitary giant in his presence. Playing to the hilt his dangerous game. And the devil take the hindmost, Jeremiah.

28:12–14 The likes of Hananiah are not granted the last word (or *in casu*, the last gesture of the drama). If such were the case, the logic and common sense so dear to the world would rule the Bible as well—a sorry prospect indeed.

And were Jeremiah merely commonsensical, and did Yahweh in this resemble the prophet—surely the Bible were shown redundant, in face of the crashing worldly logic of an Hananiah.

What need of a Jeremiah, of a Bible—of Yahweh? In the machinations of this functionary and his like, we could with ease assemble a *Protean Handbook: Instruction on the Subject of Riding High in the World.* Thus assimilating to our own interest, that formidable principality known as the "system." And this on its own terms, its own turf.

A caveat may be in order. Lest we take Jeremiah too easily to heart, or drown good sense in vain pieties, let this be confessed: for the most part, our favor (and our methods) falls not to the lorn prophet, but to the way and wile of an Hananiah. Jeremiah resists the alliance; and he stands alone.

This, we are to understand, is not a stance taken once and for all, the issue resolved, done with in time, whether evoking mute admiration—or plain incomprehension. No, it arises and arises, a kind of antiresurrection of the Beast. Alliances, more alliances. NATO, SEATO, Warsaw Pact—and NAFTA securing the slaves and markets. And the naysayers against such manifest violence, what of them? They continue to stand, for the most part, alone. Alliances of advantage continue to seduce, even the otherwise high minded—especially if such arrangements hold out the promise of a "quick fix" applied to troublesome matters.

In moments of high tension, as Hananiah demonstrates ably, a veneer of religious language is greatly useful. It is after all expected of him, the highest of priests. More, it impresses sound secular minds, for whom a mellifluous invoking of God, however misdirected toward the deity, impresses. Sincere fellow! and a spate of holy talk—what harm? (Differences duly taken in account, religious folk or not, we are at one—the alliance must be concluded.)

That standout Jeremiah. He embraces, as though the body of a lover—his helplessness, his dependence on a providence that uses him so hardly. And more, he urges on others such attitudes as stoke his own fiery, contrary way. And urges such as the will of Yahweh, and the only way to ensure the commonweal.

For every stroke of Hananiah, Yahweh has a counterstroke. This we are informed by Jeremiah, to be sure—which in a sense loads the issue. That vexed question of credentials! The two stand there in contention. And which of them is to be thought the true prophet? Who the false? Whether the vote is to fall in favor of Jeremiah or Hananiah, the credential can hardly be of his own offering. (We hear each: "I speak for God, he does not.") And we go round and round in circular argument. Something must occur that escapes the text, and so makes the point.

It comes to us gradually over the years, touching the heart strongly—a sixth sense at work? In any case, a sense that in Jeremiah dwells an unimpeachable nobility. Shall we name his crowning quality—integrity, a burning passion for the truth—a passion that ironically cannot but fall short, before the sinuous good sense of the worldly and wise?

Little men, pseudo-prophets, kings, priests, the renowned and the anonymous crowd the pages of the book. And amid the motley Jeremiah comes and goes, solitary, often stricken and downed, burdened like a pack animal with his yoke, the awful burden of being "sent."

28:15. But wait. Yahweh, it seems, has a long memory, especially regarding affronts and false witnesses. Presently Jeremiah is instructed to return and face Hananiah once more. He is to take up again the matter of the symbolic yoke, and the scene so cannily, gallingly stolen from himself. Tell Hananiah this: "For breaking a wooden yoke, you only forge an iron yoke." And worse; you are a false prophet, and have deceived the people. For this the penalty is death.

That event occurred, we are told, "that same year." End of episode.

29:20–23. We are astonished (but not really) to learn that purveyors of false hope have sprung up among the exiles as well (vv. 20–23). Two are singled out by name as criminal, Ahab and Zedekiah. They notoriously prey upon a people already victimized. So a fate worse than that of Hananiah is designed for them, their crime being worse by far than that of the hope-mongers of Jerusalem.

If, as charged, they announce to the enslaved an imminent end of exile, a dangerous memory is awakened, a futile hope. Inevitably, the Babylonian captors' ear is to the ground. And a question arises among the guardians of the slavish status quo: "By what means this end of exile? Is rebellion in the offing?" (A conjecture has it that the exiles have already caused trouble within the Babylonian borders. No more of that!)

Whether in warning or retribution, punishment falls, swift, ruthless. The king condemns the dissidents to be burned alive, in public.

29:1–10. But we need to backtrack, to that famous letter of Jeremiah to the exiles. Its content, as will be recalled, is shocking in the extreme. Hope for early release and return to the homeland is dashed to ground. And Jeremiah, without preliminaries or softening of the message, announces in Yahweh's name: "Only after seventy years have elapsed in Babylon, will I visit you and fulfill for you my promise to bring you back to this place." No help for it—and this from the only quarter they could turn to.

Strangely too, surrounded as the exiles are by a pantheon of strange gods, not a word of instruction is offered regarding worship. In Jerusalem they had despised the covenant. Can a sojourn in Babylon be thought to improve their consciences?

An awesome turnabout. Bowed as they are under a yoke harsh beyond telling, it seems taken for granted by the prophet: enslaved, they will observe the covenant with seriousness and devotion.

29:24–32. More toil and trouble. Jeremiah's letter, as might be expected, raises a furor.

One among the exiles, Shemaiah, evidently of the coterie of "return is near," sends a letter back to Jerusalem, addressed to the temple police. The effrontery of Jeremiah, his offensive urgings of assimilation in Babylon! Shemaiah inquires, with an edgy querulousness, why the aforesaid Jeremiah has not been silenced, there being public stocks available for the likes of him.

Jeremiah, far from cowed, responds wrathfully.

Yahweh has spoken. Upon Shemaiah will fall the fate of the priest Hananiah, if not worse. Not only he, but his offspring, will die in Babylon. (Evidently since the entire generation is to die there, the edge of punishment is the death of the children in exile.)

11
Against Odds, Yahweh's Love Prevails (30:1–32:15)

To Build and to Plant (30:1–31:34)

And at length we touch the high point of the prophecy of Jeremiah. The tide has turned; once more divine favor falls to the demoralized, broken people. In a sense, the poems of this section are out sequence of both time and place; they have little connection, except by indirection, with events that precede or follow. All the more powerful!

There have been hints and starts all along on the theme of "return." But the dark was so deep, deep as the maw of hell. And the dawn so long in arriving!

First, the unthinkable. The skies crashed down over Jerusalem; the bad times all but swallowed in darkness the promise of good to come. A long, heavy, foggy interlude. Belief and hope all but extinguished, an entire people flattened to ground.

Another image. Those whose fate is a mere gleaning after the harvesters are diffident of prospect and promise. A seat at the banquet of the Realm? So you say, but when and by what means? And meantime what relief is at hand, here and now? For the present, an awful wasteland stretching to the horizon and beyond, seventy terrible years—for this "present" there is no relief at all. They must make the simple, brutal best of the worst.

30:1–31:26. The prophet sets his own timepiece. These first poems, we are told, date from the early days of Jeremiah's ministry. The verses are paeans of joy, infused with a hope native to youth, a hope as yet unbruised on the Ixion wheel of the world.

The radiant promise of the verses is like a young springtime, relieving in measure the ferocious setbacks that follow, the harsh themes of reversal, scorn, condemnation, and contumely that are to dog him, year after year. Nor is his youth as yet shot forward into a kind of forced maturity, unwilling and yet submitting, commanded as he is to announce unwelcome news from on high.

In the poems, do we dwell in a "before" or an "after"? According to these sweet fictions, the awful years of exile are as though they had not been, as though vanished, whether from prospect or memory.

The first generation of exiles have been gathered to Abraham's bosom. But the new generation—What of them? Do they taste the aching grief of their parents? In dream do they walk the way of the great return? Some of these at least are the progeny of intermarriage. Are these content to remain in Babylon?

In this light, the songs of return, addressed to the remnant of both Judah and Samaria, seem subtly hortatory in tone.

30:1–9 See what I see, My people—
strange epiphanies,
reversals in nature—
men fainting in their tracks,
white of face, terrified
like women come to term—

changes, sea changes, as though
in nature's violation, men
grew pregnant, nine months gone.

My day, come to term!
See, I loose the bonds,
loose the newborn
squalling in the world!

Exiles, slaves,
indentured ones, come forth!

30:12–17 That wound of yours,
that suppurating wound
(secretly, secretly,

I followed after,
jealous, quick—
you reneging,
dealing Me double)—
I struck you to heart!

This hand, behold it,
has wrought you hurt.

I take you up,
anoint with tears
that wound of yours—
unhealed, unhealable
    by any skill but Mine!

30:18–22 And this to follow:
restoration, joy!
ringaround of sons and daughters,
dwellings, cities rising—
a second springtime!

On eyes that welled,
lips that spelled
all the lamentable years
dirge, reproach only
life's endless sigh—
farewell farewell.

Hear in stead
songs of praise, laughter
like icy streams
under noon sun benignant
temperate, flowing free!

And grave, majestic, equable
the promise I hand over
deed and warranty—
    your own
land, possessions, flocks
fig tree, vine exuberant—
your bloodline owning
no increment to tyrants.

Against Odds, Yahweh's Love Prevails (30:1–32:15)   **127**

I your God—
approach, and live!

31:1–6 Of embrace, of nuptials, is My song.
I your God, you My very
own!
Age-old love
new as new dawn.

Imagine, the sword
sheathed, at rest—
deserts blooming,
music welling!

31:7–14 Shouts of joy
pierce high heaven—
the remnant, the survivors come!

Strong, feeble,
lame, sound of frame,
women with child,
the aged, their shaky limbs
commandeered by hope—
the long march!

How different the going forth
driven like cattle
branded, herded to abattoir,
bound hand and foot, beaten
pillar to post, into
Godforsaken lands.

The One who scattered
far, wide, your goodly grain
now gathers you, My sheaf
My loaf.
    My love.

Fat of the land
yours for the asking.
    The premise, the promise
in your hands.

    Witness, you
priests, nations afar—

My sworn oath,
marriage vow, and—
wrath no more!

31:15–20 Rachel, mourn no longer
I, mother Yahweh
large in loss,
assuage your tears.
Even as you
comfort Me.

That son, the prodigal—
My heart stirs, I must
like Rachel
run headlong,
make of him—
(recusant,
slow returning,
against all chance
renewed)
firstborn of My love.

31:21–26 Idols, no more!
A new thing
upon the earth's face—

My people
encompass Me
with love unfeigned.

At long last,
you
vagabond, mismated
upon the earth
arrived at the place
(dream or reality
you know not,
reality too sweet,
too near for dream)

arrive—the place
long abandoned—
arrive—

the Unabandoning,
the Beloved
at portal
unwearied

waiting.

31:27–28 First, a promise: "I will seed the house of Israel and the
house of Judah with the seed of man and the seed of beast." Overtly
sexual the image, underscoring a new start. The second image re-
inforces the impression. The task, thankfully a preliminary one ("to
uproot and pull down, to destroy, to ruin and harm"), is accomplished.

The task of palingenesis has arrived: "to build and to plant."

Jeremiah—we have seen him and wondered and learned, he always
in the thick of events, insistent, courageous in his resolve that the
great "no" of Yahweh be honored. For sake of that honor, trials beyond number: desolation, risk of his good name, his freedom, of life
itself. Now the worst is over, the best at hand.

He too can breathe a new atmosphere, can accompany in spirit the
great chorus of return, its "yes" radiant with hope and resolve.

The "time of return," be it noted, is also a metaphor, whose trans-
lation we explore over a lifetime. For the present, we dwell in a
"meantime," our hope taking palpable form in communities living
by virtue of the promise, our way of speaking once more, as best we
might, the "yes" of Jeremiah.

And the desolation of Jeremiah comes also as a warning: too constant or polemical a "no" against the principalities, a "no" uttered
bleakly, unrelievedly, casts us into a pit of futility, draws the heart into
an orbit of darkness.

The "no" opposes the original intent. Here looms (under other
guises and words of course) the acceptability, more the accessibility,
of—death. Death that wears so many disguises, that may deceive even
"the elect."

Death the desirable, the useful, the masterful tool of "those in
charge"—in charge, as they assume, of life and death. Theirs is the
realm of the godlings, the weapons makers and hucksters, the errant
ethicians and their just and necessary wars, politicos and profiteers.
The believing community, need it be said, must at all cost stand at
distance from the orbit of the spoliators, the circle of Inferno on earth.

It is the "yes" that saves all: the "yes" uttered by word and gesture to one another, to children and spouses and friends, through work and prayer and a careful ecological sense, through compassion toward the victimized and expendable—through attentiveness also to the movements of the heart.

Thanks to Christ, one thinks, our stance before the world is less somber than that of Jeremiah. So is our gospel less somber. It must be that the two are joined: a gospel that denies death the last word, and our response, summoned as we are to dwell in Babylon. And this for an entire century, a lifetime, our own.

We were called, in a true sense, to "settle in," to intermarry and beget, to contribute to the commonweal. Even in Babylon. We work for the common good in the small ways we muster—including that "no" again. A nonviolent, costly "no" uttered in face of the principalities.

Verses 27 and 28 take up also the theme of inherited guilt (talk about a "development of conscience"! [cf. Exod. 20:5])—of punishment "unto the fourth and fifth generations." The subject arises also in Deut. 5:9. And even Moses improves the occasion, in a manner of speaking, offering a prayer weighted with a similar sentiment: the supposed reality, in the eyes of Yahweh, of inherited guilt (Num. 14:18). And so on. The notion has a long, tenacious hold, as a suppositious underpinning of the law.

Then—salvation! The genius of a Jeremiah or Ezekiel (the latter quoting the same proverb [31:29], to the same end) insists on taking a long, mortified, modifying (even mocking) look at the dread matter.

Jesus faced the like notion, imbedded in his own times. Encountering physical misfortune, the disciples are wide-eyed and credulous, at once curious and repelled, the very apes of popular culture. "Rabbi, did this man sin, or his parents, that he should be born blind?" (John 9:2, 3).

He stops them in their tracks. No hallucinatory dogma, no vagary however bizarre or inhuman, was likelier to enrage the Rabbi, and draw a more fervent riposte.

How comforting it must be, one reflects, how reassuring to one's sense of moral superiority, thus neatly to place another outside the orbit of love and hope. We are thankful for the angered rejoinder of the Savior, seeing, as we must, a like crippling morbidity alive and well in our midst, in the response of many in the churches to afflictions like AIDS.

And in the Jewish Bible, side by side with the theory of guilt and punishment, we note another current, a healthier understanding at work; and this from the first (Deut. 7:9–11). To each individual is accorded the love of God, freely given. Each shall be held responsible for personal defaults only. This would seem logical, as well as a counsel of compassion—received from on high, a common currency in the world.

If the covenant is to influence public structures, it is because the love of Yahweh has set firm boundaries, "Thou shall," "Thou shall not," in the heart of each human. In accord with this personalism, any punishment, including penalty of death, is to be meted out in proportion to personal default (Deut. 24:16). No one, under whatever pretext, is to be judged guilty of the crime of another in the same bloodline.

31:31–34. We come to the heart of the matter, the "new covenant" of Jeremiah, "inscribed on the heart." For Christians, as often pointed out, the meaning of "newness" and "interiority" awaits a fuller understanding. The new compact will be tendered by Love Incarnate, our Christ. (Tendered, one is tempted to say, and not invariably welcomed.)

One takes hope. Our hope is lodged in the noble spirits, more often than not anonymously living out the newness, the inscription of the law of love within. Behold and rejoice: the heart of Jesus, the hearts of believers—the heart of the matter.

For anything "new" to emerge, a newness that will spell a veritable rebirth of spirit, Yahweh must venture a prodigious first step.

We say "must"; the necessity is that of urgent love. And "within"; thus we pay tribute to the dynamic of the One Who Is. (Knowing that the One Who Is—is Love.)

Were not this love "that movest all things," that seeks us out, re-creates and cleanses, bestows large capacities of goodness, enables friendships, and cancels enmities—were not such love active in the world, surely we were stuck fast in absurdity, dead men walking.

A question. What if no welcome be accorded that prevenient love, if that love be despised or ignored in practice, or lost in a thicket of unmet promises and false worship—what then?

Then—stuck fast, absurdity, dead-end. And this despite the best impulses of Love, longing, moving in our direction.

So the covenant is to be a matter of the heart rather than of the law's rigor. And more: in accord with the new precept, love of Yahweh and of neighbor coincide in practice. All this is attractive, heartwarming, salubrious. A summons to the saints, to Jeremiah and his spiritual progeny—even to ourselves.

For the sake of the saints and martyrs, it must be concluded, the mercy of God prevails over wrath, withholds the arm from wreaking calamity, spares. And to see this love of God ample and free in action, we pay close attention to Jeremiah.

The text is sobering in the extreme. Only a few, a handful of disciples or friends, appear in the breach, defend, pluck the life of the prophet from the destroyers.

Meantime, the to-fro games of self-interest and ego play on. The overwhelming majority of those "in charge," whether of temple or palace, are agreed on one matter: this Jeremiah is a morbid, tedious interferer in the normal spin of power. Worse: he refuses to take seriously the Josian "reform." He contemns it, considers it a failure from the start—too little, too late. He speaks instead on behalf of a counterproposal, literally an act of God, the "new," the "covenant of the heart." (On these charges of substance, he is to stand judgment, and be found guilty.)

What then of us, living as we do in a contemporary Babylon, a crepuscular "meantime"? So little can be done. Still, of that little let us make much in esteem. For indeed, the truth and tradition we preserve, value, pass on—these are precious beyond calculation.

One thinks of Jeremiah's trust in the power of truth-telling (and truth-hearkening), knowing that the task often takes a symbolic form, requires imagination—and implies legal risk.

We too accept, as best we might, the harsh, seemingly inevitable consequence of such activity.

Then the arduous work of building community. What, one asks, would a Jeremian household look like? What of the practicalities of life together; right use of talents, resources, money? Care of children shared, assignments, chores?

We ask ourselves constantly: Can a community of conscience offer a measure of hope and light, when the public light is all but quenched, and the law of war and weaponry bears down hard? And further: When is that law rightfully binding on us? When is it to be strictly contained and challenged—or rejected as inimical to the "new covenant, written in the heart"?

That human law, we believe, is subject to Yahweh's instruction: "to uproot and to pull down, to destroy and to overthrow." Therefore symbolic, nonviolent acts of resistance are in order. Our instructor in these is Jeremiah himself—bearing the yoke, breaking the jar, witnessing the vision of the basket of figs, the signs of drought, the vine devoid of grapes. Each of these bespeaks a nonviolent effort of conscience, even as it disarms, unmasks, undermines, subverts "the system."

Nothing here of arms, weapons, malice, incitement to hatred. Nothing either of diplomacy, treaties, bargainings, and tradeoffs. The symbolic acts serve other powers, worlds, methods. They challenge the tyranny implicit in "things as they are," a bondage, a veritable metaphysic, a law of nature proclaiming: "Things as they always will be, must be."

The symbols also imply, all but introduce—the unpredictable; a something, a Someone perhaps, a lurking naysayer, standing against the absurd inflation of the spirit of death.

One who raises a hammer, who pours his own blood. Who endures the consequence.

31:35–37 Hear Me, people!

> The fixed order of things—
> day follows night, night day,
> north star, mariner's prow
> plowing the sea,
> high noon's
> magnanimity, excess—
>
> these be signs, portents;
> so long as ordinations
> govern planet and people—
> so long shall you be
> plenary, restored.
>
> Look to it;
>   if one day
> a prescient madman
> calculates to the inch
> heaven's height,
> takes measure of creation's
> central pole and pillar
> proclaiming, posturing—
> I, the measure of all!—
> that day
> doomsday!

The Land, Save the Sweet Land (32:1–15)

Jeremiah, as recorded by Baruch, undertakes a strange, apparently irrelevant (if not frivolous!), project. In the midst of a wasting war, he buys a field. Circumstances heighten the drama of the act. The city is under siege. As the assault mounts, the anger of the king against Jeremiah grows apace. He has dared prophesy as to dire events—events that, as even the morally purblind can see, are being verified before regal eyes!

We have heard the charges before. Jeremiah, it is alleged, has indulged in wild talk, undermining the morale of the besieged; he is disruptive, subversive. He has spoken of defeat, displacement of the conquered people, a corvée of slaves and exiles. He twists the knife in the royal wound. The king himself will be driven off to exile.

He has dared say (a strange, vivid, perhaps demeaning phrase): "Zedekiah...shall be taken into the hands of the king of Babylon, and he shall speak with him face to face, and see him eye to eye." We imagine how that foray into the king's future was received! How the considerable ego of Zedekiah would rear up at such effrontery, such a diminution of his greatness. Therefore imprison the upstart, forthwith!

"Therefore," forsooth. We are offered an example of regal illogic. Jeremiah is duly imprisoned; the rumble grows.

A lull occurs in the course of the siege. Jeremiah takes advantage of the temporary relief (37:12). He slips out of the city to arrange the transfer of a property to himself. Why is so much made of a simple transaction? According to the law (Lev. 25:25), the property is his. But there are deeper implications and hints; in fact, another Jeremian surprise is in store.

Yahweh and Jeremiah: they set us off balance, marvelously inconsistent as they are (at least according to our notions of what actions, turns, declensions, decrees, cancelings of decrees, moods, and shifts of mood befit a prophet or his God).

The two are like a single artist before an easel. The artist is ambidextrous, right hand and left at work, by night and day improvising on a vast canvas images of life and death, the colors and course of history and consequence. And as the artist creates, we who peer over his shoulder are hardly free to issue instructions as to the filling of blank spaces in accord with our notions—or to ensure that the finished portions do not shock!

Thus with the present transaction: in a sense, take it or leave.

In rather plodding prose, the famous story of the purchase of the field, hardly earthshaking, is recounted. Why indeed bother to record the incident at all, its only interest being that it occurs within earshot of the assault on the city? A field changes hands, we are told. If the scribe would make hay (!) of the event, it might be remarked that the prophet seems notably unconcerned as to the outcome of the battle for Jerusalem.

Yet on reflection, the episode teems with implications as to the character of Jeremiah—and the nature of prophecy itself. In the midst of the chaos of war, his city threatened with destruction, Jeremiah concludes a minor exchange of real estate. Talk about chutzpah! And be it noted that the field in question lies in Anathoth, an occupied portion of his country.

Thus the mere purchase surpasses itself. The act dramatizes the truth of verbal prophecy, bespeaks the ending of war and the resumed rhythms of peace, as spelled out by Jeremiah at the end of the transaction account: "The Lord, the God of Israel, has said that houses, fields, and vineyards will again be bought in this land" (32:15).

The action is exemplary, and recorded as such. Jeremiah has enacted a peaceable drama. Therefore peace is possible; more, is dramatized here, present, actual. Others might be moved to do the like. Peace might once more become the native ground of mind and heart, dear and actual as a bought field. And this even during a siege of terror, when all but a few are trading mortal blows, sweating through destruction and violent death, the actuality, present, consuming.

In the midst of war, a work of peace. Amid the crimes endemic to wartime (an eruption and epiphany of hell), a prophetic act declares the integrity of the human, embattled though it be—dramatizes the human, vindicates it, celebrates it!

Buy the field; declare yourself friend of creation (and of the Creator); indict the destroyers of an ecology blasted and degraded by war. And perhaps most important of all—within the boundaries of a protected zone, declare the carnage here and now and in this place, off-limits. No hand wringing, no self-pity; but a lively spirit of imagination and enterprise. In worst times we are not to play victim, not to give up, not to sigh in resignation before the invincible caissons. The action bespeaks—connections; Jeremiah, man of Yahweh, man for others, friend of creation. A soul at peace, calmly carrying out "the one thing necessary."

This, though he reports, as though from a circle of the Purgatorio: "The Babylonians have built siege mounds around the city to capture it, and they are attacking. War, starvation, and disease will make the city fall into their hands" (32:24).

Fire and sword—and then the work of peacemaking. The evil time will eventually collapse, yielding to the vision. Despite all, something more, some breakthrough, a possibility looms. Make it come true, bring it at least an inch closer! Another clue to the indomitable soul of Jeremiah.

And an analogous clue, in our own time. In 1992, the community of Jonah House in Baltimore were offered a large field in the inner city. The field had comprised an old cemetery, long abandoned. The stipulation was simple: the community would restore and maintain the cemetery, which had become an urban wilderness, untended and gone to wrack. Trees and gardens were envisioned. So was the building of a dwelling for the community.

Thus was the drama of Jeremiah once more enacted.

The community had resisted war and war preparation for a matter of thirty years; war in Vietnam, Panama, Grenada, the Gulf. During those years the members were literally "under siege." Life became a kind of Jeremian continuum; they were harassed, arrested, convicted, jailed. The imagery of the original held firm and painful; they went forth to court and to lockup, an "exile" of note. Then they "returned," in accord with the "promise."

The community learned of the connections underscored by Jeremiah: war and its domestic aftermath, neglect of the "widow and orphan." So the small rowhouse in which they dwelt became a cornucopia of gifts and goodness poured out to the neighbors. Week after week, year after year, they set about feeding the hungry. The task, the connection: "This end of the other end" of imperial misadventuring.

And now, the field, and the dwelling going up. Volunteers, many of them skilled, arrived from all directions to help. Against the odds of hard times, financial help poured in.

O Jeremiah, your prophetic soul!

12
And the Last Shall Be
Remembered (32:16–36:32)

The Deed: Small Step Out of Babylon (32:16–44)

The handing over of the deed of purchase to Baruch is a momentous occasion. Fittingly, Jeremiah marks the event with a prayer. We have here, so the experts tell us, a pastiche of postexilic phrases, with only verses 24 and 25 of Jeremian origin. Be that as it may, the prayer is nobly worthy of the good man's spirit, and thus a gift in itself—as well as for its placement here, classical, typical. Notable occurrences, that is, are to be immersed in prayer.

The law is reverenced in our testament as well. Jesus prays, whether before or after or in the course of events exemplary, symbolical, or crucial to his vocation (or to ours).

Turning to Yahweh in prayer also places the world and one's presence there, dense and absorbing as it is, for the moment "on hold"; it is as though the soul, gone too far ahead, returned to itself.

32:17–20. As to the prayer, it is a classical Jewish outpouring of praise, a doxology. Such acts are free, in the manner of God's own giving. All other considerations, whether of need, recompense, result, favor, are for the moment banished. Praising God asks only that God be God. The heart responds to the divine "first step" in our direction.

32:21–22. There follows a recounting of the "magnalia Dei." It is as though a Feast of Liberation were in progress, its immemorial question raised: "Why does this night differ from all others?" Memories, memories; the people summon a vivid anamnesis. Doing so, they bring to birth once more a formative past, the memory of the saving deeds of God. The memories thus reborn, vivid and vivifying, are as soul to the body. Through recalling them we become truly "present," to ourselves, to the events.

Or something else happens. No prayer, no remembrance. The memories wither and die; the people are reduced to a dead body in a soulless bondage known as the "present." Stuck there, they are stripped of prospect or relief. Such an unrelieved "present" becomes a one-dimensional nightmare, a moonscape of the spirit.

Condemned to it, we are victims of the perfectly sterile, chilling atmosphere of tyranny: in effect, the "one way," the "Babylonian way." It offers its captives a pantheon of icons, drawn from a culture of idols and idolaters: tycoons, military satraps, political hacks—demeaning, implacable, vulgar. And these, one sighs, are the heroes to be honored and emulated? Closer to the truth, they are carriers of death. They demonize memory and imagination, evicting the historical, tested humanism of saints and prophets.

The people are led to forget. Forgetting, they are easily led. Consumer come-on, sound bite, ad, billboard, vapid political gobbledygook, film stars and their epiphanies—these are the inducements, false promises of beatitude.

Subjected to the befouled winds of the culture, we are impelled to forget our true and native heroes, our Christs. The culture thus exacts a heavy price; it consigns us to Babylon, to a lost sense of who we are— before God, before one another, before creation.

We die the death named forgetting.

32:26–44. To counter the foregoing, we are offered a greatly expanded midrash, the response of Yahweh to Jeremiah's prayer. The prophet's impetration spells out his hope against hope—that the siege of the city can be lifted. Or failing succor, in a way that escapes his powers, that good may yet come of unexampled disaster.

Good? Come of what?

Certainly not of the assault on the city, which has occasioned disobedience to Yahweh, armed resistance. The hope of Jeremiah springs rather from a modest unwarlike act that, as he audaciously insists, held a divine sanction. Thus a modest action opened a breach in the presumably invincible forces. Because it was done in obedience.

So his act surpassed the vain works of defense. Jeremiah can say:

"You were the one who ordered me to buy the field"; more, you issued the order "in the presence of witnesses."

Year upon appalling year passed, layer upon layer of national experience, of death and massive displacement. Jerusalem has fallen. And God regrets nothing. Instead of grief, an indictment. The "holy" city is declared a "provocation, from the day it was founded."

The accusation is universal, it spares no dignity, high or low. It is like a Pauline analysis of the Fall, as the event touches on every time and place.

Summoned to the bar are "their kings, their leaders, their priests and prophets, the people of Judah, the inhabitants of Jerusalem."

Thus the Fall is seen as a transhistorical reality; it includes in the time of the prophet, another "fall": that of the holy city.

Does the latter event mark a resumption, another instance, of the genetic story? One is hardly allowed to doubt it.

Horror upon horror are detailed: the city is taken in fire and sword, the people driven afar like chaff before a wind. Social and personal crime have brought this to pass. Jeremiah looks hard at the ruins (as he saw all in prospect, in the malice that greeted his warnings).

Yet the promise remains intact. So does that modest action of courage and enterprise: Jeremiah sallying forth from the doomed city to purchase the field of his heart's desire. Who would not love him for that alone?

In verses 38 to 44, Yahweh offers covenant and field, the one shedding light upon the other. In the understanding of Jeremiah (and of Yahweh as well), a modest sign goes far and deep into reality; it touches matters high and low, divine and human, the spiritual and the visible.

That "field" is obviously of import to the intercourse of Yahweh and his friend. Among other blessings, this: it is as though a divine husbandman were planting healing realities in minds blinded and polluted by the smoke of battle.

As a symbol, the field grows and grows. It is like a magician's rug, an airborne sign—of a future assured despite all. Look up, look up!

A small slice of geography takes the guise and import of prophecy itself—a small relief in a viciously factitious world of pricings and sell-outs, of betrayals and treacheries, of greed and disregard! Cling to the field with all your might! "Fields shall be bought in this land of which you say, 'It is a desolation, without man or beast.'"

The inner eye, the eye we call trust or hope, looks farther than the desolation, sees better. The present is not all (unless despair make it so), is not the end! "People shall buy fields for money, sign and seal deeds, call in witnesses." And this, as Yahweh urges, not in one or another isolated corner, but all through the land.

The symbol is hardly static. It is a task, a labor; it implies a drama. It is as though, walking out of the burning city and completing his modest purchase, Jeremiah is weaving cables of trust.

One to another, all to himself—he is binding together the cords of Adam. Binding his besieged people to a small and precious evidence, to an ecology, a soil, a future. And this though he resides in a hectic present, as the earth groans and the heavens fall.

One would be hard put to exhaust the symbolic riches of the field. The field collapses time; it symbolizes promise, amplitude, gift, avatar, ardor, an entire land restored. Is the land blood-ridden and desolate? It shall be "a land flowing with milk and honey."

Truth in Prison (33:1–26)

Alas, the symbol falls short of understanding. The artificer of a drama of hope is stalemated, a prisoner in the king's palace. And we are told that the passage under our hand is an expanded version of his teaching. Lucky we! (Our sense of time as mere sequence, with events moving along submissively, like beads on a string, is once again put to the test. Is this the only way of seeing reality? Jeremiah will not leave us so flat of gaze.)

The commentators refer to the text as "extremely repetitious"— and let it go at that. Reading as they run, running as they read, the commentators here tend perhaps to consider themselves not so much servants of the word as its sedulous critics, even its improvers.

But why not a different tack, considering ourselves as invited to pause, to take the text whole cloth, standing on its own, requiring little of our comment?

And does not the prophet-as-prisoner add a certain weight to the passage, in somewhat the way a prison, locking one in, locks out certain ways of perceiving, of telling the time? Jeremiah has been cast out of the world. What perception of the world and his own times is open to him now? What themes become important to a prisoner, punished as he is for the crime of truth-telling? And what indeed is the "truth," judged so harshly by the powers?

Could the prisoner be revealing something of great import, underscoring it, driving it home repeatedly, inviting us as it were into his cell, into his heart and mind?

We have an analogy in the prison letters of Paul. He invariably referred to his being "in chains" as both a credential and a bond with the faithful: "My imprisonment in the cause of Christ has become well known, ... and ... most of the brethren, trusting in the Lord because of my imprisonment, have far more courage to speak the word of God without fear" (Phil. 1:13, 14). "... Praying for us as well, that God may open up to us a door for the word, so that we may speak forth the mystery of Christ, for which I have also been imprisoned" (Col. 4:3). "I have you in my heart, since both in my imprisonment and in the defense and confirmation of the gospel, you all are partakers of grace with me" (Phil. 1:7). "Do not be ashamed, then, of witnessing to our Lord, or of me his prisoner" (2 Tim. 1:8).

Could it be, in sum, that the ideas and images presented here are judged momentous by the prisoner? And by Jeremiah's close disciples as well, and by his scribe—those who grasp most closely his intent and instruction? A sound assumption, one suggests, and potentially fruitful.

33:2. We shall linger over the text, as the prisoner labored to construct it. At the start the God of creation is invoked; Yahweh is unconfined by worldly systems and unexcluded by bolts and bars. He enters and speaks with the prisoner. Majestic indeed, and moving: creation is the credential of Yahweh, his vast "second scroll," perennially unrolled while time lasts.

And likewise: imprisonment is the credential of Jeremiah, a sole and sorry one, to be sure, but unchallengeably genuine, a source of pride, certain to be heartening to believers. (In sum: "Yahweh formed the earth, and set it in place"—and formed Jeremiah; and here and now, set him in place!)

Thus is indicated, one thinks, a kind of natural consonance between the summons to speak the truth—and the consequence. Cause, effect nicely dovetailing; a logic one finds unsettling and close. Do this, dare thus—and shortly find yourself bound under the law, which is to say, find yourself disposed of in a fallen world, to whose systems the truth is judged a mortal adversary.

33:3. An invitation, and a strange one. The prisoner is to "call to Me, and I will answer you." Answer? But not, let it be inferred, in a matter that might be thought pressing to the prisoner: release, vindication, restoration of honor and status.

None of these is of point here. The "calling on Yahweh" is concerned with other affairs. And the "answering" likewise. There is a work to be done—where one is. The prisoner, for the time being, is to accept the bolts and bars, with what peace he can muster. (The implied instruction resembles the one delivered to the exiles by Jeremiah. They too were counseled to accept hard times. Now the prophet is to undergo a fate analogous to theirs.)

Call on Yahweh, he will answer. Shall we name the answer—wisdom, insight granted to one locked in a dense, unwelcome situation? How sense the why of it, even the value of it, the blessing, the example offered others? Is it a power bestowed on the powerless, a power of endurance, steadfastness, holding on?

We are in deep waters.

Still, the "calling out" as well as the "hearing" are hardly unique to Jeremiah. Prisoners of conscience, in chains, are invited to grow wise, in accord with the promise of Yahweh: "I will tell you wonderful and marvelous things, that you know nothing about."

Namely what? What we need reminding of, again and again: the power of nonviolent resistance, in prison and out.

And the caducity of worldly institutions and powers.

Those "rulers and kings and priests and prophets and citizens of Jerusalem and Judah" (how Yahweh lingers on the litany, thus battering at the rhetoric of unaccountability, presumed virtue, cover-up). They would lord it over others (lord it over Yahweh!). Willfully they persecute the saints.

The imprisonment ensures and dramatizes this: you, Jeremiah, are placed at distance from the violence all about. I place you apart. A harsh mercy to be sure. Prison is their punishment against you; it is My mercy toward you.

To such prisoners as Jeremiah is often granted, in our experience, insight into the culture that has punished them.

Such has been true of the Plowshares prisoners, as manifested in their letters and diaries. Scripture has been their burning glass, placed against the combustible funerary matter of the times. Thus they are granted to read the times aright, to instruct and hearten us as to the misuse of power, the crimes of the mighty. And so to earn our trust and gratitude. The truth has not vanished from the earth; it has only been penalized, as is the way of the world.

Is it to be wondered that, at this juncture, images of fiery destruction flame up in the imagination of Jeremiah? His imprisonment is an incendiary crime against the word of Yahweh. But his custody itself issues in a scripture. The word of Yahweh illumines his predicament. As John the seer wrote: "I am John, your brother, and as a follower of Jesus, your partner in patiently enduring the suffering that comes to those who belong to the Realm. I was put on the island of Patmos because I had proclaimed God's word and the truth that Jesus revealed" (Rev. 1:9).

As is verified anew, with our own prisoners of conscience.

THE PRISONERS, THE CAVE
To Philip and the Plowshares, 1993

> Ancients are writing with pencil stubs
> scriptures in a cave.
> What will be, what was
> is, is, is in the cave.
>
> Patience, a crystal, tells the time; that
> and a cry; How long O Lord? That
> and no reply.
>
> The parchment unrolls as they write—
> a sky, a beyond,
> a flying carpet, a throne
> whence issue thunders; Thus Sayeth.
>
> The cave is a pock on the moon.
> The moon wastes and wanders,
> a sea guarding its salt.
>
> Unrolled one day ("My Day"), the scroll
> stutters, whispers, keens, thunders—
> too low a pitch for humans
> (lions plotting
> the last day of the lamb)—
> too high a pitch (angels
> rehearsing apocalypse).

33:6–12. There is another side to the message of destruction, another "marvelous and wonderful thing…you know nothing about." It goes this way: "I will heal this city and its people and restore them to health." As before, so here: we have prophecy under a double aspect; fact and metaphor. The first is historically verified; the second is a kind of koan whose disclosing is—up to us.

As to the fact, or rather to the promised fact: the coming catastrophe was horrifically detailed; so with the restoration.

We are told of the rebuilding of a demoralized community, in a humanized landscape. Notably, the blueprint of the future makes no provision for military prowess. Quite the opposite: the "words to come true" are of the spiritual environment of the new covenant, altogether charged with "healing,... abundant peace and security,... prosperity, rebuilding,... forgiveness,...," charged with Yahweh's own "joy, honor, and pride."

And if the nations "fear and tremble," it is not because a new Babylon, lunatic and cocksure and death-wielding like the older, has arisen. Rather, it is because something utterly different has arisen, something simple and heartfelt, almost Quaker in tone: it is because of "the good things I do for the people of Jerusalem."

The metaphor of restoration—What to make of it in our day? Who believes that the principalities of death do not have the last word concerning the destruction of cultures and cities, the devastation of the landscape, and most terrible of all, the mass murder that goes by the name modern war?

A prisoner, his life thrown like a random seed into some tyrant's dark pocket, believes it. Of what worth is he, or for that matter, his absurd faith? Has not the tyrant (here, be it noted, no "lion come down," but a domestic banality)—has not such a one already had the last word?

And yet, and yet. We are given pause. The book we ponder is not entitled the "Works and Pomps of Zedekiah," or "The Book of Hananiah the Prophet." Instead, the title of honor, the story and its crown, are given to another. The petty churlish ruler and his puppet-prophet hold a place in history solely as the dark eminences who inflicted suffering on the prophet.

They vilified and sought to destroy him; they live because of him.

Thus does God delight in reversing the field, tumbling the thrones, turning words of pseudo-prophecy topsy-turvy, shaking out the seams of existence. Jesus also delights in the reversal of fortune in many works and words; and his mother also, in her great inaugural hymn of roles reversed, the Magnificat. And Jeremiah is their ancestor-brother in the spirit.

Those great ones, how they are brought low. No lasting place, no admiration or affection for such, except through their victims; discredited they stand, shamed before history.

Nor is it recorded that God promises the Zedekiahs of this world that "I will tell you wonderful and marvelous things you know nothing about." (Could this be because such eminences could hardly admit to "knowing nothing"?) The promise belongs to the prisoner, reduced, defamed. The last shall be first.

A liturgical chant is heard, plaintive and yet strangely triumphant. Clearly, the prisoner's spirit is unbroken. The sound of thanksgiving echoes down the centuries, a psalmody—Psalms 100, 106, 107, and the refrain of 136: "Give thanks to our God, who is good, whose loving-kindness is everlasting."

To whom belongs more fittingly than to this one (who forsook family for lifelong friendship with Fire, for treading of Fire)—to whom of greater right belongs "the voice of joy, the voice of gladness, the voice of the bridegroom and the voice of the bride"?

It comes to him in prison, in silence, in solitude, desolation of spirit. He hears the voice of Yahweh, telling of a future healed and restored.

The voice is literally beyond words; it comes to the prisoner as a music of the spheres, a song of the Maker of spheres; a music nonetheless of our earth and its bridal beckonings from worlds beyond.

Ecstasy is the gift to the one who has risked and lost. And shall find.

Jeremiah, that man of mourning, here surrenders to—joy, intense, fierce, the fruit of valiance. For years the range and ravages of his emotional life expanded wonderfully, raised and lowered and raised again on high, peak to pit. In nothing spared, in no gift lacking.

He lives all the more intensely for being the organ of the passionate, jealous One.

33:14–26. Two realities are closely joined in biblical history, and in the concerns of Jeremiah no less. He would have the Davidic line and the levitical priesthood both continuous and integral. The prophecy is redolent of confidence, despite the ruinous times. A just one will come, will guarantee in his person the bloodline of the spirit; and justice again will flourish on earth.

More: on that seedbed of historic crime, Jerusalem, so beloved, so betraying, will be conferred a new name, "Yahweh, our righteousness."

It must be recalled constantly to mind—the promise.

We too have been known to lose heart in evil times, under the soft savagery of the culture (and not so soft after all; consult the people subject to bombings at our unsoft hands, then to throttling "sanctions").

And the declared enemies of the empire are by no means the only ones assaulted. Against us also wars are declared, even though in a different form. This form: the dimming of vision. Wretched actualities intrude, a persuasive cast take center stage. They bespeak and enact the only drama playing—we are told, the only one worth attending to. Its title: "The Way Life Goes"; the only way, by plain implication—or now and again by overt insistence.

To dream of another way, a different one, a biblical one, is both fruitless and (possibly) dangerous. You long for a Moses? Consult the outcome that befell certain among the dreamers of "another way": Martin Luther King, Malcolm, Romero, the Jesuits of Salvador. Others than you have written the script; it is not to be tampered with. Neither is the staging or decor. Others than you direct the drama, produce it, underwrite its considerable financing. Others enact it. Your assigned role: applause, attentiveness; more: passivity, craven acceptance.

It is as though God had given up, as though the world were no longer worth even the tribute of wrath; as though we humans were given over, tooth and nail, to our own devices, grisly and squalid by turn; as though, indeed, the awful thirteenth chapter of Revelation were being enacted before our eyes.

The Beast makes war on the saints (but that has always been the fact); only now, a carnivorous victory is celebrated: "It was allowed... to defeat them" (Rev. 13:7).

Prophecy, today? It plays out in jail cells and death rows and torture chambers, out of sight, out of mind. But does this, our tale of conflict and defeat, differ greatly from the story of Jeremiah and his like?

Once more, a strange encoded version of time, freed from the stereotype of "before and after," invites us to a like freedom. The urging is of confidence—and this in a future by no means realized. (Undoubtedly, we are informed, the text is the work of a later compiler.)

In any case, a promise is boldly juxtaposed to the somber accounts of ruin.

It is as though in a no-man's-land battered by opposing armies, someone were cherishing a garden of roses (in evil times, we live by signs). As though a resister whose name we know were to slip the bonds of a siege laid against his city, and emerge safe, and travel apart. To buy a field.

That field of Jeremiah. It is as though, its owner absent, imprisoned, the land were nonetheless tended by solicitous hands, watered, planted, and harvested, all in due season. Who are the unseen husbanders, cherishers, ecologists? How dare they? while all about—other sounds, other hands hotly intent on other works, works of darkness, destruction, folly, contempt, the gentle land blasted to a desert, the smoke of wartime chaos.

Verses 19 to 25 instruct: we are to be comforted that day follows night, and night day. This is an observable fact, and more: a sign. The rhythms of nature stand firm; in a kind of covenant, Yahweh held an agreement with day and night, that they keep to proper sequence.

So we are reminded and encouraged; another form of order, not observable, a matter of "promise on My part and trust on yours," also stands. And this is a pledge, a guarantee: "Your kind will perdure."

And the promise, be it noted, will bring forth generations of the virtuous. Thus the shameful past is surpassed, in the quality of the leader to come: "My righteous one will execute justice." Then a worthy priesthood: "...to offer burnt sacrifices."

It appears as though all is in place, an ideal humanity is assured. And then—the awakening.

That time of promise and renewal—how it is delayed and delayed! We survey our world in dismay and disbelief—perennial selfishness, greed, violence rankly flourishing. What of that promise, that dawn purportedly nearing?

Nearer our point (and that of Jeremiah): How fares it with those of the survivors who finally returned from exile and reclaimed the land? Alas, the displacement, the generational suffering, seem to have wrought little change of heart. The old vices reassert themselves: injustice, uncharity. Old realities reappear, to no one's honor: the rich arise; the poor sink.

The promise delayed is the promise betrayed. A kind of vicious circle curves and closes; a serpent swallows its tail.

Shall everyone be engorged?

A mood of pessimism descends like a cloud. And despite all, the promise, like a voice from the cloud, is heard: "I will restore their fortune and have mercy on them."

The Scroll Alive, the King Extinguished (34:1–36:32)

34:1–7. We hear the first of three "words," evidently drawn from the memoirs of Baruch concerning the eventual, long-awaited restoration. This word concerns the fate of the king, as the second siege of Jerusalem proceeds. Zedekiah has been commanded to pursue a policy of peaceful surrender; only thus will city and king escape, as Jeremiah has repeatedly announced (chaps. 17–38).

It goes without saying (or perhaps it does not) that we too are offered (also repeatedly) in Jeremiah's life, evidence of nonviolent response to violence, and this to a heroic degree. He takes with utmost seriousness the urgings of Yahweh, a contrary pressure against the violence so characteristic of the kings—urgings that invariably are ignored, contemned in practice. Except for the lonely one.

We are told nothing of the outcome of Jeremiah's message to the king. One is bemused. Why not? Why leave so important a matter suspended? Is it sufficient for the purposes of Jeremiah's glance into the future that the message simply be put on record—and left to a more hopeful time? With the possibility that meantime, humans will undergo a measure of moral improvement?

Is the hope that (and here we touch on hope against hope indeed, a hope that contradicts awful evidence of perfidy), at long last, some generation (even ours?) might be led to take the hope of Jeremiah seriously?

34:8–22. A lengthy second word of the prophet recounts a shady, indeed shameful, deal. The setting is the besieged city. For once, King Zedekiah seizes the initiative, ordering a general manumission of slaves. His motives are left unexplained, but by inference they would seem not particularly elevated.

To wit: either the siege brought such hardships as made it impossible to feed the slaves, or the city's defense (violent presumably, and in contravention of Yahweh's will) required an increase in the phalanx of warriors. What better expendables at hand than a slave population, recently and grandiloquently set free—free to die that is, and be killed?

In the first hypothesis, the newly freed will be forced to fend for themselves as to food and lodging. In the latter, the "freeing" only served to implicate the "freed" in a vast network of socialized disobedience and sanctioned killing. Some freedom!

Nonetheless, we are told, the charade went forward, polluted from the start. The slaves were ceremoniously set free, in accord with ancient covenantal instructions. From these (Exod. 21:2; Deut. 15:12) the law is clear.

But here, the manumission, combined with a formal covenantal ceremony ("You made a covenant before Me in the house which is called by My name"), underscores the solemnity of the occasion. So solemn a sacrifice is described only once in the Hebrew Bible—in Gen. 15:9ff. Here it is merely referred to.

But there as here, animals are slain as substitutes for the lives of parties to the compact. Should these latter prove unfaithful, the animal corpses dramatize the parties' own destruction.

Clear, painfully so: "And I will give those who...have not fulfilled the words of the covenant which they made before Me, when they cut the calf in two and passed between its parts,...I will give them into the hands of their enemies" (32:18, 20).

The crisis in the city passed. And without delay, a monstrous betrayal occurred. The former slaves were once again taken in custody.

Yahweh is outraged. And Jeremiah comes forward, a very lion of retribution. He plays upon their cruel charade, turns the infamy like a blade against their own throats. Have they been pleased to indulge in a preposterous charade of "freedom"? Very well then, Yahweh shall set the perpetrators "free"—so to speak. "I will set you free; free to die by war, disease, and starvation."

Another irony: they have violated a law enacted of old, in relief and remembrance of their own slavery. Just as they were liberated from Egypt by an act of God, so every seventh year, they are to liberate those who serve them. But the slaves are again enslaved. Now (can such be imagined?) it is as though God reneged on Moses, handed back their prize to the Egyptians.

35:1–19. The curious tale of the Rechabites (and the bearing of the tale a bit later). This is a tribe of believers, we are told, their devotion to Yahweh frozen in time and place. O but faithful they are to the minutiae!

So, Jeremiah is instructed to invite them into the temple, to offer a dramatic lesson to priests and people alike. The issue is the Rechabites' abstention from wine; but the small refusal is enlarged, as questions of more import arise. We picture them, these foundation stones of an old order. Rather clumsy, willful, even ironbound, entirely honorable— heads held high, they enter. It is our largest glimpse of them in the Bible. (Originals, first generation Quakers, Mennonites, Shakers?)

In just a few sentences we learn much. The Rechabites are nomads; they conceive of Yahweh as a God of nomads. They fail to understand, let alone embrace, the lure of the land, the temple, homes, agriculture, commerce. They would identify such settled accouterments and occupations with—a Baal whom they resolutely reject. Sheer, literal obedience, letter of the law! For this they are praised and rewarded, in the temple, in full view of another sort of folk—the recusant Jerusalemites. What a contrast!

And now (in vv. 12–19) for the purport of the episode. The predictable instruction follows. These tribes people obey Me, you do not. Therefore catastrophe.

We have seen it repeatedly. Nothing is more straitly insisted on in Jeremiah (or, for that matter, in the prophets across the board) than the connection between moral irresponsibility and the collapse of a culture. Including a religion absorbed by the culture.

The above scene, as could be predicted, is taken badly by the congregation. What people, especially if they be commonly regarded (especially in their own estimate) as godly, would not be aroused to a fury when the suggestion is aired that their godliness is open to question?

The persecution of Jeremiah intensifies. Accountability is at issue here, and consequence.

The entire episode we owe to Baruch, faithful as always. Now, along with his mentor, the fidelity of the scribe is put to the test. He too must face the wrath of the king.

The two have dared predict, not only the wrath to come, but its source—the crimes of the mighty. (The implication of the wrath that falls once more on Jeremiah is plain. There must be only one history, approved by the mighty makers and breakers of event. So the prophetic attempt to set down the truth is received as a plain threat. The infamous scroll of Jeremiah must be destroyed, and the truth-tellers put to silence.)

The timing here is important to both sides. For Jeremiah and Baruch, it is crucial that their account hold firmly a double aspect.

First, it must delve into the past and review the prophet's warnings, the tale of conscience and courage, neglected, despised, ignored. Second, their scroll must be timely, unmasking recent delicts. It must unroll with all deliberate speed, close upon the wake of event.

A prime example. In the very heat and smoke of a war even now underway, their account is a judgment; it must summon authorities to the bar. For the war is in clear violation of covenant and of prior instruction, repeated like a drumbeat (or a heartbeat): no war, not even of defense!

For the king and his kind, timing is equally crucial. Timing of a different sort. Their version of history implies the exact opposite of Jeremiah's. A waiting game is their strong suit: at all costs, keep the truth under wraps, as long as feasible. Buy time, bribe, cajole, keep mum, pay for silence; this for years, the longer the better. Eventually, those who mounted the war will either be removed from office—or dead.

And by then? The truth is defanged; all parties to the crime run free. For who takes seriously a toothless tale, the stuff of folklore, grown old and harmless? Time is "on our side."

If the dossier can be closed for long enough or concealed—or best of all, destroyed—crime and consequence will be judged of no account, will be refuted easily, with a sneer and smile: harmless, an old wives' tale.

Against the leveling tyranny of time, little avails. Long after torrid events have cooled, biographies, histories, doctoral theses, "investigative reports," all purporting to shed light on obscure matters, clog the market. In vain their claim to the truth. The myths prevail.

The day of the locust knows no sunset. Thus the old age of scoundrels, prospering to the end.

Chapter 36 is a wonderfully expressive and vivid passage, equal to or surpassing other sublime narratives of the Jewish Bible. We are there; we witness a scene of regal perfidy.

Rumor flies fast. Fascination, fury: everyone, it seems, is shaken, must hear the contents of the infamous scroll. Three readings in a single day, to three diverse audiences! The account of Jeremiah and Baruch is hardly lengthy; but what thunders it looses on the air!

36:3. The spoken word of the prophet has gotten precisely nowhere; so let us try another tack. Write it down! A scroll implies permanence, a record available now and in the future, an enduring judgment. A threat as well: what is read publicly is also on record; it is not so easily dealt with!

36:4. Baruch appears here, a character of great nobility and courage, as shall be seen—and a true friend, one who believes passionately, against the mad current of the times. Like a John the Baptist announcing a greater, Baruch—modest and practical—is willing to all but disappear in his own text. This is to his glory, and our immeasurable advantage. It is he who plucks Jeremiah from the mass grave of historical anonymity.

Were the will of the king to prevail, we would have no record of the life and word of Jeremiah. Nothing but the version—official, colorless, lying, and laudatory—confabulated "from above" by the palace claque of scrivener-prophets. But the design is thwarted. How far, how lasting in effect, a single act of courage! Baruch preserves the narrative of Jeremiah and passes it on and on, down the ages into our hands. For this inestimable gift, all thanks.

36:5. To Jeremiah, the temple is a forbidden area. The prohibition is obviously due to his sermon (7:1ff.) and the episode of the broken jar and the valley named for Slaughter (19:1–20:6).

Still, daring, nimbleness of mind, courage—these will come up with other strategies, other ways to proceed. Baruch stands with him. In effect, Jeremiah to Baruch: we shall together write the history of these years. Then hie you to the public court of the temple and read it aloud. And this on a major feast, when large crowds are present. Then we shall take our chances.

One delights in it, the derring-do of prophecy. Try this, try that; improvise, move swiftly, with brio and finesse.

And the truth will out. Or will it?

36:9. An entire year of labor, and the scroll is finally complete. The occasion is ripe. But will the tactic succeed?

We are not given to know, nor are the courageous protagonists. More, it seems as though even Yahweh knows little or nothing beforehand of the outcome. "Perhaps," he says, "when they hear of the destruction . . ." (always that threat—and might it be ventured, not the best way of proceeding?), "perhaps they will turn from their evil ways." Or perhaps they will not.

But in any case, the courageous conspirators set to work at the tactic proposed.

36:10. Baruch proceeds in a public place to unroll and read; loud and clear, as may be imagined. The scene is electric with danger and opportunity. This is no dead scripture, long intoned and droned. The ink is hardly dry. The words are raw and incendiary, hot with dangerous truth, an eyewitness account of crime, reproof, judgment. Was there ever a reading like this, a scripture like this? A ripple runs and runs through the crowd in attendance. And then widens, further and out.

36:15. Shortly, official ears prick up. Their owners send for Baruch, and demand a second reading. Before them only. It astounds, appalls, angers. The king himself is indicted; he must be told of the infamy.

They hotfoot to the palace. Outrageous Jeremiah is about his old ways, O king! beyond rehabilitating, this recusant, self-willed recidivist. The king's cronies enlarge on this latest delict, and insist soon on judgment and condemnation (38:4).

It is wartime; the argument of patriotism vs. subversion of the "national effort" runs hot and fast. "This man must be put to death inasmuch as he is discouraging the men of war who are left in the city, as well as the people. . . . He is not seeking the well-being of the people, but their harm." The king lends a ready ear. The scroll, he is informed, accuses him again and again. He is the architect of national intransigence, the builder of ruin, the adamant warrior of refusal.

36:19. Certain among the officials are troubled by the gathering wave of fury.

On the one hand, the scroll dares impugn the king, an act unheard of. (More: the tragedy of hapless Uriah is a recent memory, and a bitter one to some. The king's vengeance has a long arm.) Some among the officials, perhaps a remnant of the older administration of the king's father, intervene to protect Jeremiah and Baruch. Go hide!

36:21. Stony of visage, the king orders a third reading of the nefarious scroll! The reading is periodically interrupted.

36:23–26. As though the narrative were a branding iron applied to his flesh, as though, driven beside himself, the king must seek relief: "As soon as Jehudi finished reading three or four columns, he cut them away with a small knife and threw them into the fire." The scene is one of appalling cynicism, an effort to destroy history, to bring the truth to naught.

Like father, unlike son! Baruch's scroll, by artful implication, contrasts the reaction of King Josiah as the law was read to him. The former ruler conceded the delicts of the people, and took holy resolve on a sweeping reform (2 Kings 22:11–20).

What is the dark hope of this pitiful, arrogant scion? Perhaps to expunge the record of his crimes? Seemingly, the royal intransigence knows no limit. To the crimes adduced in the scroll is added another: the burning of the record.

Act and symbol once more. "Neither the king nor any of his officials showed a sign of sorrow" (v. 24).

Two camps, seemingly irreconcilable, face off: the king and his court, on the one hand; and Jeremiah, with Yahweh adduced as sponsor. The message of the prophet is plain; he has repeated it again and again; until, one thinks, even the dead must take note. The instruction of Yahweh—it is ringed about with a fiery threat. There is to be no armed resistance against the Babylonians; or all is lost.

Over opposite, the king and his cohorts dig in, determined on a contrary course of action. Jerusalem must resist the invader; counter-violence, ideological unity are the order of the day. No dissidents allowed! The citizenry, one and all, must be drawn into the war preparation; then into the war.

The city of God, the all-too-human city.

War erupts, minds slam shut.

Jeremiah and Baruch, the only channels of mutuality, of message, of access to a wisdom other than that of the warrior-king, are artfully isolated. They are put to silence. Yahweh the Dissident is put to silence.

The city gates are shut. We all but hear the great hinges drawing together ominously in their sockets. Beyond reconciling we, whether with God or one another?

Conflict, and the dual way—war vs. the command to forebear war.

The situation in the city worsens; the Jeremian thunders fall like fresh rubble about their ears. The king "cannot bear very much reality" (T. S. Eliot). Does the arrival of an evil time, hauled in like a siege works, show the rightness of the prophet? Shall the king, under such evidences, undergo a change of heart?

He will not. As in every war, illogic is in the saddle. The words of Jeremiah verified before his gaze, the downfall of the city imminent and then accomplished—these serve only to close the royal mind like the great city gates, to stiffen folly to an obsession. He orders the arrest of Baruch and Jeremiah.

But "the Lord hid them."

36:27–32. We are reminded: the king burned the books; he burned the Bible. Is this the first book burning of history? In any case, there is a terrifying, punitive forthrightness to the scene. We note hatred, intransigence, a ferocious, choleric rejection of the truth.

Willy-nilly, the king who would destroy scripture is herewith included in scripture—as fact and parable. He has earned his dubious eminence—by burning scripture—in-the-making. And lo! despite his wintry fires and hot furies—we have in hand the scripture he sought to destroy. And ours, alleluia, is an emendated, more complete version than the one he set afire!

Ours. To have, to hold in hand, to ponder. To live by. Including the strong indication that worldly power and the word of Yahweh make for an incendiary mix.

Nothing daunted by the fiery stoking, Jeremiah and his friend undertake another edition. This one will incorporate the narratives of the first, adding to them by way of serendipity, the king's frenzied reaction, the burning.

So the episode ends.

But it never ends, to this day. We have before us that second edition of Jeremiah's scripture.

The king's winter fire is long extinguished. In that fire, in a vain gesture, he sought immunity from judgment. Like his fire, like his vain assault on the word of God, the king too is all but extinguished—a near nobody, a petty tyrant, raving, wreaking, tempestuous.

His fretful, childish gesture, futilely standing against God's word, is cast in vain against the winds of truth. Pity him.

13
A Life of Fidelity:
Scorned and Rewarded
(37:1–39:18)

Wartime: Justice Flies the Coop (37:1–10)

As the Babylonians prepare to take charge in Jerusalem and Judah, we have yet another king, this one a vassal appointed by Nebuchadnezzar. In the estimate of Jeremiah, he does not amount to much, a pliable weakling. Weakness on high, strength below; the ironies of Yahweh in full play.

An interruption of the siege. The Babylonian armies fall back under a threatened invasion from Egypt. (The same event occasioned the shady deal regarding the Hebrew slaves [34:8ff.].) So in the hiatus, a delegation from the king waits on Jeremiah. He reports his own situation somewhat wryly as "not yet put in prison, still moving freely among the people." The message is a curious one: "to ask me to pray to the Lord our God on behalf of our nation."

What is he to make of the message, and its sudden outburst of piety? Ambiguous, to say the least; Jeremiah has reported that "neither Zedekiah nor his officials nor the people obeyed the message which the Lord had given me."

To all appearance, the "message" has to do with that famous second scroll, its intimations (and more) of the morbid outcome of national apostasy—specifically, of catastrophe on the heels of disobedience. The new king is a prime vacillator. He indulges himself in an ambiguous devout gesture, even while the war proceeds on schedule. (The schedule as to timing and method is Babylonian to be sure—but the Jerusalemites by no means turn to nonviolence.)

We are forced to fight! (How often have we heard the reasoning.) We are under assault; defense is legitimate; ours is indubitably a just cause!

As to Jeremiah, might he be thought to turn God around, just to a degree, just for this time? To assent to the logic of king and people, to bless the war and its courageous warriors, thus to shore up the "national resolve" (a mighty Fortress etc.)? No such response. O unequivocal naysayer!

The king, to put the matter charitably, is a slow learner. Can he be ignorant that from the start of the siege, he had his answer, Yahweh via Jeremiah (34:1–7)? What need, then, of the tardy request for the prophet's intercession? Alas for the king: beyond all control of his, events are moving swiftly in the direction of Jeremiah's word.

How then stem the tide? He stands like the mad king of the legend, knee deep in swamping waters, commanding them to recede. He receives a response—stern, telegrammatic. In the national wound, a knife is twisted. This: "Let us suppose the impossible, the routing of the besiegers. Even granting this, even supposing that the Babylonians had at command naught but wounded soldiers—still these would rise and bring down the city!" (37:9–10).

Stark, vivid, a text visible to the purblind. But it floats past the royal eye; weakness breeding obsession. A lull in the siege, no change in the high command of defense.

Jeremiah resolves to take advantage of the momentary peace. He departs the city once more, to visit his newly purchased property. Alas for the untimely move! Whoever dares move about freely is on the instant suspect. Jeremiah is accosted. Do not all true-believing-patriotic-citizens belong in place, "contributing to the war effort"?

He will make no such effort. In illustration of an alternative, he will pursue a normal peaceable activity: the overseeing of his field. Thus declaring in effect (and this surely is the rub): the siege and its attendant madness are hardly to be taken seriously by a believer, one who has received, and conveyed, the will of Yahweh in the matter.

Indeed in departure from the bloodletting, he renounces it publicly: it merits nothing of attention—still less of blood.

Or Jeremiah might be saying: I seek—enjoyment. I would feel the earth under my feet, unpolluted by blood. I long to plant crops and grow and harvest them, to taste the joy, the serviceability, and sweetness of creation. Let me pass.

The war, on the other hand, your war, is—a sanguinary mirage. It bespeaks the quest for a spurious glory. I will have none of it.

Halt! He will not pass.

Normality, morality, these are in short shrift. It is wartime, the normal and moral are—suspect.

He is detained. He has a bad record, even in peacetime. And now that the purported "word of Yahweh" is all but stifled in the chaos engulfing the city, may he not, in retribution, go over to the enemy?

War: suspect the worst of one another, and act on it.

War: constrict heart and mind, let lethal fictions prevail, stifle the good sense that creates alternatives.

The unrehabilatable peacemaker is taken in custody once more. This time, the punishment is doubled: he is beaten. "I was put in an underground cell, and held for a long time." A prisoner of conscience if ever there was one.

All thanks to you, Jeremiah, all honor to your stripes! (We note too that the house of the court secretary has been altered in use; it is now a prison. Another "temporary" conversion of normal usage, made expedient by wartime?)

There are ominous hints that the "justice system" is out of control. The king gives over judicial decisions to subalterns. He "sends for" Jeremiah; no investigating his case, no questions asked as to the abrupt, brutalizing punishment.

Once more, the query is loaded with self-interest: "Any message from the Lord?" The pieties barely conceal the unease; the real question would go somewhat like: "What is to become of my royal person?" (All very well that you, Jeremiah, are a prisoner, your crime unexamined, your punishment altogether arbitrary.)

Jeremiah is no mincer of words. He disposes of the king's craven inquiry in a single sentence, devoid of comfort: "You will be handed over" (as indeed, the irony, you have handed me over). Then Jeremiah raises, as he must, the question of his own fate. What was his crime? How comes it he is held in custody, and for how long? And what of those lackey-prophets who deceived the nation with their prattle about "no attack on the city"—have they also been punished?

Logic, quest for justice? It is wartime; justice has flown the dovecote. The prisoner knows it; the knowledge overwhelms him. He breaks down, ends with a heartrending appeal: if you send me back to the dungeon, I will die there.

(One commentator all but melts in a puddle of admiration at the king's response. No justice, be it noted, no calling to accounts those who summarily jailed and flogged him.

(None of this, but a sop, a modicum of mercy, a mitigation of the rigors of imprisonment. Jeremiah is transferred to "the palace courtyard," and given a bit of bread.

(And the learned comment goes: "The secret interview ends on a fine gesture of the king, a sign of his love for the prophet."

(Come now. It might be ventured that our exegete somewhat resembles the king, a moral meliorist; half a loaf, so to speak, an improvement on—none.)

Unearthed and Unbowed (38:1–28)

38:1–5. Toil and trouble. The word of Jeremiah is unfaltering. And the reaction continues to be—awful.

A storm gathers once more. The good man is reported to the king, evidently by poursuivants. In the presence of the ruler, their tone is remarkably arrogant. They are strong in wickedness; the king, they judge cannily, is wickedly weak.

It is of interest that the words of the prophet (v. 2) are an accurate (but according to Jeremiah, incomplete) report of his supposed criminal themes. So (in v. 3) he (or Baruch, it comes to the same thing) boldly interjects and amplifies the quotation. And thereby, of course, compounds the crime! "The Lord told me to say also that the city would fall."

Under the law of the jungle, this is criminal speech. Let us suppose a jungle, with beasts. And a crisis. Who is to own what? Various claims are urged on the part of the lesser beasts. The claims are denied. The great carnivores come together, in defense of what they regard as their common provender. No matter what their differences in normal times, here they are one. A declaration is issued against the presumptuous. We have a name for the above phenomenon, as it exists and flourishes in our midst: war.

Let us spell out the criminality of Jeremiah.

He has indulged himself in a siege of his own, counter to our war, has attempted to divide and confuse, with his fearsome "thus says Yahweh," our seamless phalanx of minds and hearts. Or perhaps he has not succeeded in creating dissent; he is still in violation, the point of the law being precisely—the threat. In effect he is a turncoat, if not a collaborator with the enemy.

The accusers are apparently a law unto themselves. No quotation from the law of Moses is offered in support of their condemnation; clearly, none exists. In their books, as they shortly undertake to play both judge and prosecutor (and would cheerfully play executioner), the crime is a capital one. They urge the death sentence.

What malice, long hidden, has gathered to a head! Jeremiah, it shortly appears, is expendable. The king surrenders him to his enemies.

The placing of the episode is masterful. Both before and after the exchange between the detractors and the king, Zedekiah summons Jeremiah. Who is in command here, who the prisoner, who free?

The king appears torn, unstable, now cozening, now raging. He detests the prophet, but is childishly needy, clutching at some small approval of his course. He is a great wringer and washer of hands, a veritable ancestor of Pilate, of the line of bureaucratic masters of expediency. A moral zero, he creates a vacuum into which malice rushes. The spies sense it; his weakness is their strength. Zedekiah confesses as much: "Jeremiah is in your hands; the king can do nothing against you."

Such as Zedekiah, weak, unprincipled, whining a dirge of powerlessness, know nothing of fidelity or friendship. They betray; their trade is in human lives. Let a Jeremiah (or a Jesus) be hailed before them, one whose sandals they are unworthy to fasten, whose nobility is a rebuke: such will shortly be found—expendable.

38:6–13. The sentence is a capital one. To have the troublemaker perish at the bottom of a more or less dry well is a malign stroke of genius. Jeremiah will die slowly, of exposure or starvation, or both. No evidence will point to the executioners; no marks of violence or bloodshed on the corpse.

Against all odds, Jeremiah is saved. The savior is a person otherwise unknown, but surely of remarkable courage. The word is abroad, a news sure to be found embarrassing to royal ears: Jeremiah has been flung into a well.

Our friend proceeds to beard the king as he holds court at the city gate. How to respond? Ever wobbly, the king performs another gymnastic flip. Suddenly he is all solicitude, bustle, showy resolve. The messenger is to take with him three others: forthwith, they are to draw the prophet forth from his ignominious tomb! And Jeremiah is summarily plucked from, so to speak, death row. His future however is uncertain; for the present he remains a prisoner, "kept in the court of the guard house."

38:14–28. So we arrive at the last of these bootless exchanges between Jeremiah and the king. This is their most extended dialogue; and psychologically, of greatest interest. Dominant in Zedekiah's style is the artful dodging known to its practitioners and admirers as "statecraft." Jeremiah's response differs remarkably. His speech is suffused with moral transparency.

Beware the powerful who belabor their "love of the truth." The king desires only the truth, he avers. Jeremiah: for the "truth" you are willing to kill me; and as for advice, you will never heed mine. The king: I swear it, you will not die at my hand. We note that in the matter of accepting the prophet's advice, the king utters not a word. Nor will he, ever; a clever sidestepping of the issue.

Zedekiah, in effect, wants it all. Consider the irreconcilables, his determination to square the circle. He wants his war to issue well, and he wants the compliant favor of Yahweh. Granted, he has in his hand's palm a coterie of housebroken prophets. They readily assure him of "no problem." But their glib blessings bring him no peace. Again and again, in panic, he seeks out an incorruptible presence, a will that runs counter to his own. If only Jeremiah would concede, ever so slightly, this small point: that the king's purpose merits divine approval!

He will not. Not now, not ever. The king may cajole, threaten, cozen, stonewall, betray, as this or that advantage dictates. All to no avail.

The matter of "no war" is a capital one. Jeremiah holds firm. In him the original promise of Yahweh is fulfilled to the letter; he has become "a fortified city, an iron pillar, a bronze wall." Zedekiah's fortifications are as nothing compared to this.

Repeatedly the message drums away: no war, the will of Yahweh. Has the king gone deaf? Deaf or not, let him look to it; he shall either cease and desist from the carnage, or the wrath of Yahweh will bring him down, he and his house of Atreus.

Half-unhinged, suddenly the king shifts course (vv. 19ff.). At least for the moment, his fear shifts away from the Babylonians (he has never of course feared Yahweh).

Another dread overtakes him: that his sweet skin may suffer at the hands of "those of our countrymen who have deserted to the Baby-lonians." A new tack, and a strange one. The illogic of a nightmare possesses him. Waves of fear and torment toss him now here, now there. He is like a Macbeth in midst of a mental breakup.

Nor can it be missed: to him questions of faith and obedience do not occur. His life is an open invitation, to the manipulation of the wicked. Were Jeremiah unprincipled, he could mold the royal clay to his will.

To the king, this prophet appears as a kind of mirror image of him-self. The mirror, it goes without saying, is weirdly distorted. The king sees what he sees, his glance highly selective, a filter apt for a needful ego. So seeing and not seeing, turning away to semblances, he misses the reality of the one who stands before him, Jeremiah, man of faith and obedience.

Zedekiah seeks a potent magic, a medium with access to this or that god. He reasons within himself: a prophet is a magician, a juggler of events, a fantast, suggestible, guileful.... Surely such a one is open to proffers of enlightened self-interest....

He wants the deity, all that Jovian power, at his side. Strong magic! Thus the king's conception of Yahweh, and of the usefulness of Jeremiah.

Let the prophet then urge that Yahweh fight alongside his own, ensure "our" prevailing. Only choose sides, in the manner of the pantheon of Greek and Trojan gods!

It is all absurd and pitiful, the perfervid lucubrations of a brain gone awry. As to a good outcome for himself (to Zedekiah the heart of the matter), and dependence of that outcome on his surrendering the city, the king will not yield. At this point does Jeremiah give up, turn away? Persuasion, logic, threat—all have failed.

He does not turn away; he breaks into song, as though he would soothe a feverish child (v. 22). The words, we are told, are drawn from an ironic song of the day, portending certain events. Covertly, for cold comfort in time of war, someone, some Brechtian spirit, his hand on the public pulse, has composed a song. And the embattled people sing along, knowing the code.

The war rumbles near, if it is not already underway. A sense of fatal-ism hangs on the air. The most grievous burden, whether in casualties or starvation, will fall to the shoulders of the people. The king will eat; so will the generals.

One image of the song is striking; Jeremiah surely finds it delicious.

Has the unknown composer connected his near demise in the well bottom with the predicament of the king?

> His feet are sunk in the mud,
> his friends have abandoned him.

The siege grinds on and on. And among the populace, gallows humor; the forbidden song is heard everywhere.

Canny Jeremiah! He incorporates the ditty into his own vision; thereby, one thinks, uniting two unlikely worlds: bawdy verse and the exalted will of Yahweh.

His "vision" goes this way, as he describes it to the king:

> The women of the palace are led out to the officers of the king of Babylon. As they go to their fate, they sing:

> > The king's friends betray him,
> > a puppet they play him;
> > muddily he thrashes about,
> > a coxcomb, a lout.

The exchange, like every prior one, reaches an impasse (vv. 24–28). The king dwells in darkness and the shadow of treachery, his mind whispering intrigue.

Macbeth again, as though Jeremiah can be inched into a corner where a Macduff grows complaisant. Nothing for it, the king says; if their conversation is leaked, both parties are at the mercy of restive "advisers." Let us then resort to "damage control"; of this meeting let nothing be said. Jeremiah agrees. Why not? He has failed repeatedly to "catch the conscience of the king." And he himself remains a prisoner, nothing of his status ameliorated. Why then risk further punishment?

Vindication (39:1–18)

39:1–10 Fire and sword and the end.

And the terrible beauty of vindication. Jeremiah's worst forewarnings have come to pass. The matter-of-fact account masks his heart's grief, a heart long since broken on the wheel of the world. Broken and, despite all, mended.

How many times has the city fallen? How many times must he suffer the ordeal? And ourselves as well.

The forbidden scroll bears us like passengers of a rudderless craft, hither and yon in time, back and forward, in and out of repeated tellings, in anticipation, in awful images of fire and sword, in the insistent voice of Yahweh ("Tell him...! Tell them...!"), in repeated warnings falling on deaf ears, in unendurable suffering.... The years, the years of Jeremiah. They are Pauline in range and rage and moral scope, in the ironies that stretch the soul on a procrustean bed. Jeremiah, like his great descendant, stays the course and endures the consequence.

Paul enumerates the costly litany, a grand organ burst of rhetoric, a poetry of terror and grandeur: "...giving no cause for offense in anything, in order that the ministry be not discredited, but in everything commending ourselves as servants of God, in much endurance, in afflictions, in hardship, in distress, in beatings, in imprisonment, in tumults, in labors, in sleeplessness, in hunger, in purity, in knowledge, in patience, in kindness, in the Holy Spirit, in genuine love, in the word of truth, in the power of God; by weapons of righteousness for the right hand and the left, by glory and dishonor, by evil report and good; regarded as deceivers and yet true, as unknown yet known by all, as dying yet behold, we live; as punished yet not put to death, as sorrowful yet always rejoicing, as poor yet making many rich, as having nothing yet possessing all things" (2 Cor. 6:3–10).

And O the prophetic soul! The litany of horrid events plays on: utter ruin of the city, sacking and pillaging of the temple, blinding of the king and execution of his sons, driving forth of the great ones.

A month passes. The fallen city is silent as a hecatomb. And off the exiles go, over the horizon. Off the edge of the earth? In any case, a caravan of misery and hopelessness. And who are left behind? What are their prospects? The poor and landless and unproductive ones remain, leaderless. A colonized tribe of survivors, eking out an existence on the scorched land.

Not a Moses (not a Jeremiah!) to be seen.

39:11–14. And then—a truly Grecian reversal of fortune for Jeremiah. Who would have dreamed it?

In service of the truth, at the hands of his own, he has endured harassment, imprisonment, corporal punishment, threat of death. And come the conquerors, the pagans. Utterly ruthless to his opponents, they surround Jeremiah with solicitude. By order of the great king he is immediately released, and put under the care of an officer, "to see that I got home safely"—home to his beloved field?

A Life of Fidelity: Scorned and Rewarded (37:1–39:18) 165

39:15–18. A résumé, a look backward, a merciful touch amid the chaos: "While I was still imprisoned... "

The identity of the savior is out! He is the same Sudanese eunuch who rescued Jeremiah from the well. Yahweh, we are told, "remembered" Jeremiah. Which is to say, Jeremiah remembers his benefactor. And proceeds to reassure and reward. For saving the prophet, the Sudanese will be saved; the destruction of the city will leave him unscathed.

14
All That Fall (40:1–45:5)

The story of Jeremiah continues. In chapters 40 to 44, we are offered an account of his fate after the fall of Jerusalem. (By common agreement, we owe much of this to his friend Baruch.)

Jeremiah Freed (40:1–6)

The Babylonian captain arrived in Jerusalem one month after its fall (2 Kings 25:8). His charge is an ominous one; he is to put the city to the torch, and to organize the caravans of those marked for exile.

With regard to Jeremiah, we have a notable exception to the common fate. The king has learned of the "doctrine of submission" on which Jeremiah had vainly insisted. (In verses 2 and 3 the scribe quite remarkably places a summary of the teaching on the lips of the military officer.) In consequence, Nebuchadnezzar issues an extraordinary order of exception. The prophet is to be dealt with humanly; he is left free to choose his own future.

Will he accompany the officer to Babylon (not, to be sure, as an exile, rather in the way of an honored guest)? Or would he prefer to remain in his own land? "You have the whole country to choose from; you may go wherever you wish." Astonishing, an utterly unheard of courtesy. He is offered, of all things, choices.

For years, his people have disowned him, repeatedly and with fervor. To the end, to the last letting of blood, they have feinted and dodged and disobeyed his commands.

It is as though a cultural death wish had prevailed. They chose to lose it all—the truth of their place in the world, the covenantal blessing, the temple, the holy city, their land and freedom—in favor of a demented willfulness. Now many are slain, the living exist in such misery as to envy the dead. A multitude issues forth into slavery and exile.

And the truth-teller, long despised and put to naught, walks free, honored by an otherwise implacable enemy.

The story of the Fall comes to mind, verified once more in the behavior of an entire generation. Darkness of intellect, we are told, seizes on the mind, a weakened will puddles and pollutes strong resolve. And a squalid communal outcome is held to lip—a cup brimming with fire and blood.

Jeremiah's future, for a vast change, is in his own hands (v. 5). And he is struck speechless, this man of many words.

Is it the kindness of his captors that confounds him, or the utter newness of his situation, brimming as it is with promise? Is he to be free of the yoke of prophecy that galled his shoulders for years?

The commander seems to sense the situation, and offers a suggestion. Let Jeremiah stay for a space with an old and trusted friend, Gedaliah of Mizpah, whose family had previously (26:24) sustained him. This Gedaliah was placed in charge of a provincial town, Mizpah, the administrative center of the invading regime. (One wonders: Is he to be thought a collaborator?)

He has probably chosen the only possible course. The Babylonians are apparently willing to allow a small colony, a remnant, to settle in the environs of Mizpah. These are the landless, the poorest of the poor; they are uneducated and unlikely to make trouble for the new masters.

Gedaliah offered himself as a mediator between the settlers and the invaders. (Subsequently he is appointed to a high post, governor of Judah.) Meantime, word of the concession of land gets about, and Jews from other regions gather in Mizpah. Life on the land resumes a peaceful course of planting and harvesting—for awhile.

Jeremiah, Parable of the Word (40:13–43:13)

40:13–41:3 (cf. 2 Kings 25:25). The remnant are left to themselves; a kind of garden-of-innocence atmosphere prevails, even in a formally occupied country. Deceptive, disturbing even. Then a tragedy erupts, shattering the pacific beginnings of the new regime, the benignity of the (distant, not particularly oppressive) tyrant.

Gedaliah is of noble spirit, intent, it seems, on the well-being of the remnant in his charge. Treachery is brewing. He is so informed. And as is so often the way with personages of his quality, he waves the reports aside.

Names are named, proffers even of preemptive murder reach him. He will have no part in such a jihad. And his own goodness proves his undoing. At a banquet held in honor of newly arrived guests, in shameful violation of the laws of hospitality, the host is assassinated— by a "Macbeth" named Ishmael.

It transpires that all the guests at table had knowledge of intent, and conspired in the murder. Brigands unmasked, they run amok in the town, slaying both Judeans and Babylonian soldiers "who happen to be there." As can be imagined, grief and consternation arise all through the occupied territories. Each year henceforth, the stricken people will commemorate with a fast the death of noble Gedaliah (Zech. 7:5; 8:19).

41:4–18. The slaughter at the banquet and afterward is a prelude to further horrors: "mere anarchy...loosed upon the land." We are given no clue as to the motive of the butchery. Bloodletting has its own peremptory law; it spreads, a widening circle of violence.

To this degree of ferocity, the violence: a group of eighty pilgrims dressed in mourning garb were en route to the ruined temple of Jerusalem. They passed near Mizpah; wrong place, wrong time. Ishmael the assassin lured them into the town; there they were brutally murdered. Speculation has it that he coveted the offerings of "wheat, barley, olive oil, and honey" carried by the pilgrims for offerings at the temple site.

How will the slaughter be received by the Babylonians? Blood will have blood. The terrifying series of episodes, a conquered people wielding the sword against one another, is taken by the occupying power as an act of subversion. Will such be tolerated? Heavy threats of reprisal hang on the air. Now only a remnant of the remnant survives; they reach a desperate decision. They must flee to Egypt, the only neighboring country free of the Babylonian yoke.

42:1–18. The ragtag band of survivors is strangely reminiscent of the caravan of misery that departed Jerusalem years before. Into Babylon were driven the high and mighty. Now, another smaller exodus, all the more pitiful for its few and lowly members! They pause for a breathing space near Bethlehem.

In the blur and bloodletting of previous events, Jeremiah all but disappeared from view. Now we are brought once more in his presence. He walks amid the new exiles, bereft like them, burdened by the common plight, fallen silent. What now of him, we wonder—What of that shining prospect of peace? what of the field he so longed to walk and work? All vanished, a mirage.

At one inn where they pause overnight, the pilgrims, "soldiers, women, children, eunuchs," approach Jeremiah. Deeply moved, one looks them in the face; hapless, helpless they are. They have lost and lost; they are the least and last, the expendables, perennially displaced, homeless, unwanted. Shall we say (with perhaps too easy a pity)—how little they had to lose? Still, there survive connections, memories that must be thought precious—temple, relatives, friends, home, and country.

Their city burned and sacked, they were strewn about the land like ungathered straw after the gleaning; of no great value to the angels of death. Then they must witness the multiple murder, the hand of their own raised against their own. And finally they flee once more, brands plucked from the fire—but in view of what future?

And now they approach Jeremiah. What, one wonders, has been their connection with him, in the years before the war? They or their fate have never been a matter of political significance. They were no kingmakers. They had no part, were granted no part, in the vile decisions of the great ones—those who contemned the prophet and undertook the war.

What a contrast they offer, suppliant, apparently obedient to God's will, in contrast to the high-handed king and his ilk! Jumbled together in a sack of misery. Their only commendation: their predicament and Jeremiah's are alike. So they approach, seeking the intercession of the prophet: "Pray for us; intercede for us; learn God's will and we will obey."

To speak of literary skill, the episode is consummately arranged—in view of an absolute shock at the end. We are led along (perhaps Jeremiah was so led)—to a conclusion that seems both logical and just. Imagine. At long last, Jeremiah has come on a people who hearken to the word of God. Would it not appear that suffering has brought to birth a far different congregation, disenfranchised as they are, without a stake in this world? And one notes that the initiative is theirs; they come imploring his help.

So we are led to believe as they approach, making a great point of dutifulness: "Whether it pleases us or not, we will obey the Lord to whom we are asking you to pray."

What to do? For ten days, Jeremiah tells, he sought the will of Yahweh in their regard (in his own as well). What is the next step, where are they to go? Ten days' delay; and the situation ever more tense, the fear of Babylonian vengeance mounting.

And then the answer, harsh and clear. Strange, how familiar it sounds, in many ways equivalent to the earlier command forbidding the war. Word of Yahweh: There is no salvation in Egypt. Egypt too will be overrun.

They are not to proceed; they are to halt and turn back. And a promise follows; the imagery we heard from the beginning is voiced again: "If you are willing to live in this land, I will build you up and not tear you down; I will plant you and not pull you up."

A word, better a cry, follows. It is as though wrung from the heart of Yahweh—or the heart of Jeremiah: "The destruction I caused you has brought me great sorrow.... I am with you" (42:10–11). No accusations, no threats.

Astonishing (but we have been astonished before!): the attributing of their suffering by Yahweh—to himself. It is as though the disasters that brought them low were contrary to his will, as though their guilt were being placed in question by a new onrush of compassion.

All said, these poor ones had no part in the wrongheaded decisions of the great.

And yet they too were caught up, swept away in the whirlwind, cast down, a detritus. And Yahweh is filled with sorrow, and remarkably apologetic.

42:19ff. Jeremiah knows it, in his bones. Does he read their faces, their eyes?

He has not yet heard a response to his "word of Yahweh"; and his bitter wisdom anticipates their hardness of heart; "I warn you now, you are making a fatal mistake. You asked me to pray for you, and you promised..." (42:19).

Appalling. They are unchanged after all. Their suffering has brought little or no wisdom. The pieties and niceties of the "little ones" are one with the willfulness of the great ones.

43:1–4. Sin, we learn, is no preserve of the powerful. The powerless are also sinners. Suffering can harden as well as convert the heart. Like a serpent shedding its sleep, the "original sin" insinuates itself, raises its head in this encampment of misery as it did amid the splendors of

Jerusalem—pure, fanged, a poison. They ape, all unwitting but equally benighted, the mighty ones. In effect: We will not obey.

And more: You and your cohort Baruch are lying in your teeth; Yahweh would never issue such a command as you palter (43:2, 3).

We are appalled and enlightened at once, though the light has a look of darkness within. Against our instinct (perhaps against the last-ditch hope of Jeremiah as well) we slog alongside in the caravan of misery. And willy-nilly, we listen and learn.

Once again, Jeremiah loses. It is borne home to him: there is to be no relief. The hideous cliché of evil is like a century plant; it will bloom and bloom again. His life is closed before it closed; failure is its gnawing motif; it will eat him to the bone.

Misery too creates arrogance. The leaders, we note, are too canny to take on Jeremiah directly. They aim their shafts at the defenseless scribe: "Baruch has stirred you up against us, so that the Babylonians will gain power over us, to put us to death or exile us to Babylon" (43:3).

Empty bravado. The leaders beckon the remnant; they set off. Direction: Egypt. Baruch and Jeremiah are unceremoniously swept along. Now he knows it. Rejection is universal; it depends neither on class nor status nor the worldly predicament of "his" people.

Was there ever such a suffering servant? The last chapter of his martyrdom is being written. Beginning, middle, and end, turn where he will, to memory or prospect, it will be the same—despisal, scorn, raw contempt.

(In this, Jeremiah much resembles the Peter addressed somberly by the risen Savior. Age will grant no respite; in his last years he will be harshly displaced: "When you are old, you will stretch out your hands, someone will bind you and take you where you have no wish to go.")

And no separating the fate of Jeremiah from the fate of God's word. This is a capital point, the horrific implication here: Jeremiah's is a mirror of God's fate in the world. The life of the prophet is a parable, a portal to a larger, more terrible event. His failure signals the rejection of the word; of the will to reject, even to eject, God from the world.

Jeremiah batters in vain at the portals of human pride. One man's fate, the fate of God. Jeremiah's is not to be thought a solitary or unique tale, concerning one king or one people. A larger story emerges—the constant drumbeat of history, signaling the arrival on the scene of yet another renegade and unredeemed generation, "kings and princes, priests and people." Ourselves.

The refugees make large claims of obedience. In effect: "We have learned the error of our ways; we are resolved on conversion of heart!" Concerning ourselves too, the dolorous truth is other than the claim. The evidence is undeniable, of the perdurance of idolatry, violence, greed, the trail of debris that marks a rake's passage through sweet creation. Truth is, we humans are in the way of learning very little from the spoliators who preceded us, whose depredations soil the pages of our Bible—and our century.

We are born into the world—fallen; a matter that bears both personal and social implication. We inherit institutions; often we set to work modifying or reforming them. And for all the goodwill we can muster, even for rare infusions of integrity and moral genius—even in face of the heroism of our martyrs, the institutions resist; they stand firm. They take on a life of their own. They exact service, then servitude. Like the fabricated monster of Frankenstein, they turn upon creators a ruthless face, a claim. They too, we learn, are fallen. Only give them time, give them a lifetime, and such entities enlist, better ingest—humans.

One thinks of the Pentagon, that impregnable principality, of the crowds who enter its vitals each day, grist for the hungers of the Beast. Millions more, near and far, are in servitude—researchers, engineers, scientists (a class, strikingly enough, who in the time of Jeremiah would be found useful in Babylon, and marched off to exile).

In our time this elite cadre, brainy and well rewarded, feed off, even as they feed, the gormandizer of death. Are these to be thought masters of their fate? They serve the Beast; they dwell in Babylon.

The all-but-unbearable realism of the Bible, the drama of the human, the inhuman, our mystery and makeup! The generation that bore transcendent Jeremiah also bore the despicable Zedekiah, the mass murderer Ishmael, turncoats like Azariah and Johanan.

Nothing, if we can credit the story, no circumstance of weal or woe, guarantees the emergence of an enlightened people. Some walk in pride; some fall to rise again; some fall and fall. Misfortune brings some to heroism, hardens the hearts of others.

Thus biblical anthropology presents us with a veritable Shakespearean cast of villains and heroes, rogues and saints. Make of it—hearken, learn, reject, embrace, rebuke, contrive—make of it what we will!

The book of Revelation recounts a series of catastrophes in nature, then holds up before us the outcome—a crazy mirror, a moral freak show, a mess and menu of foibles, sinfulness, raw hardness of heart. "The rest of humankind, those who had not been killed by these plagues, did not turn away from what they themselves had made. They did not stop worshiping demons, nor the idols of god, silver, bronze, stone, and wood, which cannot see, hear, or walk. Nor did they repent of their murders, their magic, their sexual immorality or their stealing" (Rev. 9:20, 21).

And as though the point, once made, must be driven home: "[The people] were burned by the fierce heat, and they cursed the name of God, who has authority over these plagues. But they would not turn from their sins and praise his greatness" (Rev. 16:9).

One life saves. Through such as ourselves even, tatterdemalion, untidy as we are—still, interwoven like a thread of gold is the moral uprightness, sweetness, elegance of spirit, consistency, of a Jeremiah, or a Jesus.

43:8ff. At length the refugees arrive in the city of Tahpanhes. There, to signal a future whose approach he alone knows, Jeremiah performs the last of his dramatic, public acts of resistance. Before a government building he takes stones in hand and buries them in mortar. "And make sure," the command of Yahweh goes, "that some among the Israelites see you."

To mark the place of an irony, an infamy. They have come to the wrong country in a wrong time, to a city that will offer them no peace, no security, no future.

Mark it well, Jeremiah. Near the imbedded rock a Babylonian tyrant will erect his throne. Then he will seat himself, a sign, a sovereign seizure; the conquest of Egypt is complete. A telling, ironic metaphor: "As a shepherd picks his clothing clean of lice, so the king of Babylon will pick the land of Egypt clean, and depart victorious."

A few stones stuck in mortar—marking the grave of God's hope? Marking as well a sorry vindication of the prophet, once again too late? Godly activity in the world, given the world's ways, is invariably puny and tardy, and perceived by few.

Nevertheless they are visible, those stones, a sign. A later scripture will command a newly healed man to perform another, equally dramatic sign, "as a witness against them" (Mark 1:44).

43:11. Shortly, Egypt too will be reduced to a colony, pillaged and humiliated. What then has been gained? The expatriates have gone their own way; in so doing they have amputated the future.

A sense of doom, almost of fatalism, afflicts Yahweh, as he ponders the multiplied follies that end here, in yet another doomed city, a temporal and spatial dead-end: "Those fated to die by disease will die by disease; those doomed to be taken away as prisoners will be taken away; those doomed to be killed in war will be killed in war" (v. 11).

This is the chilling atmosphere of the Fall. The holy, saving will is frustrated; the "safe haven" will shortly prove a trap. Their own hands have sprung it.

Truly a high point of our Bible. On the one hand, the proffering of Jeremiah: choices that guarantee dignity and freedom. On the other, the Realm of Necessity: the empire, its wars, its voracious appetite for death, its dooms, dooms, dooms, like bells of passing or drumbeats for the dead.

Anonymous and despised—those who fled to Egypt, those driven to Babylon. Both are henceforth indentured to time and this world, bound to the wheel of empire.

From Jeremiah to John the Divine, a throttling unfreedom is underscored as the outcome of sinful choice. Empires enslave; they would hold us in bondage, even as Yahweh would have us free.

In what surely seemed an end-time, when the Beast of Rome was loosed against the saints, a latter-day prophet took the words of Jeremiah to his lips: "Listen, then, if you have ears! Whoever is meant to be captured will surely be captured; whoever is meant to be killed by the sword will surely be killed by the sword."

And a crucial comment follows, a midrash on the earlier text, going beyond Jeremiah to celebrate the fidelity of a community of faith: "This calls for endurance and faith on the part of God's people" (Rev. 13:9, 10).

A Fitting End (44:1–45:5)

44:1–19. In Egypt the new arrivals show no hint of conversion; quite the opposite. The idolatries that cracked the heavens over Jerusalem continue apace in the "cities of refuge."

We have here two versions of events: that of Jeremiah and that of the exiles. According to our prophet, the disasters that have befallen are the noxious fruit of idolatry. The people, however, women and men alike, counter this version boldly.

Astonishing, their argument: it is precisely because the worship of the "queen of heaven" was eradicated under King Josiah that sorrows multiplied in Jerusalem. The emotional passion of the argument indicates how deeply rooted the practices were. The "queen of heaven," it is adduced, brought all good fortune; the worship of Yahweh brought only setback. A chorus of women and men joins in the argument; the women win the approval of their husbands for their part in the rites (here, "vows" [cf. Num. 30:7–16]); they shape "cakes in the form of the queen of heaven."

The long discussion underscores a spiritual darkness that can only be thought of as generational. In Egypt, subject to conditions that might be thought inductive of conversion, the people renounce nothing of the past. They drag along the baggage of the past, persisting in the ancient idolatries.

44:20–30. Jeremiah issues a last oracle of doom. We have heard it before, this tit for tat, in which wickedness contains the seed of judgment. Judgment on Jerusalem, judgment on the exiles, judgment on the civil strife among the survivors, judgment on the disobedient passage to Egypt—these are the heartbreaking themes.

With this denunciation, Jeremiah disappears from his own book.

A Christian tradition has him stoned to death by his own, in Egypt. The end seems bitterly fitting.

45:1–5. The oracle that follows, named "the consolation of Baruch," offers a cold consolation indeed. Significantly, the passage is contemporary with the writing of the scroll (chap. 36), the second edition that followed on the burning of the first. According to speculation, it is placed here so that the biography of Jeremiah will not be interrupted.

Baruch echoes the plaint of Jeremiah in the earlier stages of their work together. And no wonder: he was drinking from the bitter cup of his master and friend.

"Are you looking for great things?" or, "Are you looking for special treatment for yourself?" (v. 5). Apparently, Baruch had sought a mitigation of the sentence passed on Jerusalem and Judah.

Alas, the prayer was impossible of granting.

Thus ends the first great section, the proper "book of Jeremiah"—proper, that is, to his self-revelation, the biography of (in his own eyes) a seemingly bootless life.

Seemingly only.

Offered against crushing odds is a lifelong fidelity; substance and reward, both.

15
Oracles against the Nations
(46:1–51:64)

So we enter upon the second great division of the book of Jeremiah, the "oracles against the nations."

Technical questions of authenticity and the like need not detain us. Sufficient to recall that in the matter of the ethos and behavior of superpowers, Jeremiah is at one with his lineage; all prophets turn a fiery gaze on the "nations."

"Judgment is Mine!"

The empires are weighed in the scales of Yahweh, the scales on which the prophets weighed their own leaders and people—and oftener than not, found them wanting.

Judgment yes, and fierce; and the primacy of judgment is of enormous import. It is basic to a grasp of prophecy itself. Which is to say, the constant drumbeat of accountability falls, first of all, on the chosen. No exemption is allowed; no excuses suffice. The excuses, be it noted, are commonly based on prerogatives attached to status of being "chosen." There follows, in a tawdry logic: chosen, therefore beyond, above accountability.

The divine logic is otherwise, and quite austere: chosen, therefore all the more accountable!

The eye of Yahweh falls on his own, and rests there in discomfort. So the entire first part of the book lingers over the theme—judgment against the chosen. No lengthier, more detailed, and passionate diatribe exists.

And the response? Oftener than not, hearts are further hardened. Let God (or his prophet) rave as he will, goes the riposté. All the more determined shall be the rejection of the indictment!

The response is all but hallucinatory in its will to silence, discredit, destroy this tormentor of conscience, Jeremiah.

History, Strangely, Belongs to Jeremiah (46:1–49:39)

It would seem, from the chapters that follow, that the entire social organization of the world has gone mad. Nothing is excepted. Every known kingdom is portrayed as a vile *massa damnata*. All peoples are a blur of clones, alike as swarms of killer bees; in the midst of the swarm, treachery and violence buzz away.

The first oracle against Egypt is typical of those that follow:

46:1–28 War upon war and
             no resolution—
        battle after battle and
             no peace!

       Muster the soldiery,
   incitement, shouts;
         glory, glory!
   Dulce et decorum
         pro patria mori!
   Rise in full flood,
       armies, rise
     like a Nile cresting—
        the push of a tidal wave, and
         we inundate the world!
          Like Jehovah's shoulder
        topple
   godlings to their knees!

   Balm in Gilead?
        What heal-all
        soothes this wound of yours—
          Cain's blade
            against meek Abel,

blood reeking, tears of Eve
upon the innocent, upon
fratricidal fury.
O My people,
from chains, from yoke,
from bondage, from the cup of gall—
from the cusp of hell—
I rescue,
I race to your side!

Sown to four winds of chance and mischance, the people of Jeremiah are all but disappeared. "All but"; but for Jeremiah and his like, Baruch and a knot of disciples. These too are seeds, cast into the earth, cast into the furrow of the future.

So there is a recurring motif of hope as well. Goodness is not entirely extinguished. This, though the Beast makes war on the saints—and even is allowed to defeat them, as we have noted before (Rev. 13:7).

Let those who walk the world in faith, take warning—wounds await, perhaps mortal ones.

And yet, death is countered, stalemated. Let it be shouted aloud, again and again. Despite all, the cry of the saints is of triumph. History belongs to the Jeremiahs. It is they who offer a credible icon of the human. Granted, few among them survive to see the fruit of their suffering and labor. But something better than longevity in the world is their gift from Yahweh. They live, and die, in faith.

Another angle to this awful announcement of the "defeat of the saints": How comes it that we have before us the story of Jeremiah and of others like him? How comes it that the narrative of their "defeat" is not likewise destroyed? Their faces shine from the text, bathed in aureoles of light; their lives enliven our souls in awful times. Immersed in defeat and death, the saints triumph strangely. They offer an irreplaceably truthful version of history and of a human way, underscored with the testimony of their blood.

And what of the tyrants? These invariably fall short of their implicit goal: to wipe troublemaking goodness from the face of time and this world. To announce themselves as an "only way," a way of bravado, greed, necrophilia, betrayal, morbidity of spirit. This is their fate, a fall from glory. These anti-icons are indicted, judged, and stripped of credential: by the saints. In testimony of this, we have from Jeremiah, Daniel, Isaiah, Ezekiel, and the others, the word of God.

Suppose for the moment that God did not exist, or had washed hands of a tribe literally beyond redemption (as far as our fate is concerned, no God or a God who abandons spells one and the same predicament). Suppose that human goodness has vanished entirely; no more Jeremiahs to grace us, to prod, to allow no quarter, no hiding place, even to lash us about, to speak and speak again the unpalatable unwelcome truth.

Two conclusions would follow, with regard to our present material: (1) The oracles "against the nations" would be redundant, useless, opaque to understanding. Their judgment would be discredited by the "facts of life," facts defined by the empires themselves. If evil alone comprises the human, there can be no "evil." (2) The note of hope that so often accompanies biblical judgment would disappear from the text. Why modify, mollify, mitigate, the horrors of crime, with what amounts to a counter text? No sense to it, let horror be all.

As for the "people to be consoled," these would long since have disappeared in the mass of high culture—wars, greed, glory—swallowed whole, down the gullet, the imperial matrix. This, in sum, an obituary of the human itself. No other exemplars or icons, only the official clones. None but the assimilators and assimilated, the yea-sayers and the party line, the good lockstepping citizen-warriors, the misleaders and the misled; all and one, the "dwellers on the earth."

As in a Beckett drama, stuck, up to the neck in the encroaching muck of time and this world.

Welcome, Inferno.

Hail then the prophet and his harrowing of hell, the reminder to the victims in highly charged, passionate code: your masters are hardly omnipotent, your plight is redeemable, your sins forgiven, your survival assured.

And yes, your liberation is imminent.

> 46:27, 28   My people, have no fear.
> Far and away you languish—
> near, look, at hand am I
> to rescue, restore, redeem!

Our prophets, as we note, delight not merely in the juxtaposition of opposites (wicked authority vis-à-vis vulnerable truth-telling), the delight is in—the clash, the crisis, the reverberation, the high drama of original choices, whether foolish or exemplary.

Thus in a drama of faith and faithlessness, a great light is struck, for our sake as well. We hold the light to a mirror. We see—ourselves.

The crimes of the nations, the hope of the saints. Light and darkness, Daniel and the mad kings, Jeremiah and his opponents.

If the nations rage, it is all in vain; hope beats on.

One after another the empires are summoned to the bar. In a breathtaking departure from official norms, the stroking of kings by their sycophants—no more of that!—and long-standing versions of "official" history are discredited, toppled, then scuttled.

We read and wonder. Perhaps we take heart, even grow wise.

It is as though the ghost of Jeremiah haunts the corridors of power. Have the mighty ones succeeded in striking him down, throttling his voice?

They have not: his ghost walks abroad in immemorial judgment, through the witness of disciples and scribes and martyrs, those upon whom generation after generation, the cloak of the prophet has fallen.

Vengeance on the Empires (50:1–46)

50:2 &   The prideful city, bowed in mourning,
passim   silent as Rachel's tomb.
              My hand passes
over lutes and flutes and harps—
over the lips of the living
crimson with wine and song—then
silence.
              Bread, circuses, days of
wine and roses
Finis. Obit.

              A hand
pours the stirrup cup, proffers it—
adieu, great city
profligate of blood and money
warrior, minister, master of fate—
a pale horse awaits its rider;
destination?
              oblivion.

              My hand—
one push, like a child's toy

the squared blocks of Babylon
yield to a rubble.
   My hand
upon the idols
fools' gold, dust to dust.
   My hand
swings the great midnight
tocsin;
    twelve strokes, then
time in its tracks
   stops short
  for all time

50:4–5 After all, after the worst,
after weal on woe multiplied—
see, my people—
turn, return to Me;
"Where O when shall we
kiss once more in face
Zion's eternal hills,
fair meadows, cataracts
falling, falling
sweet, undiminished?

When,
  pledge word and will
to Yahweh,
  no other service?"

50:8–20. Understandably, the years of exile and enslavement accumulate in fierce emotional intensity, spilling off into such verses as these: red with unstanched blood, fiery with the spirit of vengeance. And the fury takes religious form: the Babylonians are "scapegoated"—by Yahweh!

And we have a strange turnabout, whether in the mood of God, or in the mood of a people whose fate has been cast on God. It appears now, toward the end of the exile, that Babylon has become the evil empire par excellence. The slings and arrows of Yahweh, formerly reserved for the Judeans, are launched against the oppressor.

The king is no longer "My servant," the executor of divine retribution against the "chosen." Sword, famine, disease are to fall on

Babylon. Vengeance against Jerusalem, once lauded as *dignum et justum*, will be avenged. Yin and now yang; Babylon will suffer the fate of those she crushed.

Here we have prefigured the Revelation imagery: "a woman seated on a red beast that had names insulting to God written all over it..."; "On her forehead was written a name,... 'Great Babylon, the mother of all prostitutes and perverts in the world'"; and "the whore, corrupting the earth with her immorality" (17:7).

This is all quite puzzling. The litany of denunciation includes Babylon, but is by no means exhausted by that entity; all kingdoms are equally guilty; all are to suffer a like fate. Thus emerges in our book (indeed in every prophetic book) a common attitude of Yahweh (and of Yahweh's oraculars) toward those political, social, economic grandiosities called "imperial," "empires."

More, and this is a matter of underscoring and repetition in the texts: it matters nothing at all whether this or that among them has been pleased to name itself "chosen." What draws the divine lightnings, obliterating all such claims, is quite simple: insider or outsider, their communality in crime. More specifically, their frenzied warmaking—including the wars they deem "defensive, just."

There can arrive no good outcome. Yahweh delivers them over to their worst instincts. Let the world (the world he created: there is always great insistence on this primal sovereignty)—let that world be bathed in blood!

Let the ungodly (literally) claim to own, dispose of, destroy at will the creation (bogus, flimsy, fractious, bloodletting as the claim is)—let it be stated boldly, acted out with all speed and fury. And this, be it noted, repeatedly, in every century. Nothing learned, nothing repented.

Let violence, which of itself knows no boundaries, which is blind and indifferent to its victims as a flung stone (or a launched smart bomb)—let it be unleashed, be itself, be "horsemen, all four" on rampage (Revelation 6).

Thus in images both violent and vile, the immoral consequence of the Fall is dramatized, and the moral nature of universe is vindicated. In a sense both universal and consequential, that "nature" of ours, despite all evidence to the contrary, is—nonviolent. So is our God; and in this above all are we to be accounted godly. Or not.

In this direction are we summoned: to refuse, to resist the killing kings. In this to become fully human, vocationally responsive.

Jeremiah is a master dramatist. His dramatic symbols push before the people and kings the matter of "no getting around it," "no getting away with it." Where and when violated, the moral universe demands, by the law of its being—vindication, "vengeance" taken. Which is to say, demands restoration of moral balance.

So he will put the yoke to shoulder, shatter the clay pot, wear a filthy rag, and so on.

And as far as Babylon is concerned, let the empire own the first act, let it pillage and rampage as it will. And then—let Babylon fall, its inner contradictions coalescing, mounting to the breaking point, its topless towers becoming, so to speak, top-heavy.

The empires are scrutinized in turn—Egypt that "country of no refuge." (We have seen the dream of the exiles, to discover in Egypt their haven, how the dream dissolved.) Then Babylon, the magisterial symbol, the many-splendored marvel, whose glories and swift demise haunt the believing community—image and substance and warning of the end-time (Revelation 18).

Then Philistia and its powerful coastal cities; Moab, ancestral enemy of Judah from the time of Exodus; Ammon, whose king wrought the murder of Gedaliah the just; Edom the plunderer, laced with rejoicing at the fall of Jerusalem; the Syrian cities controlled by Babylon; the Bedouin tribes of the desert, their vulnerable "city of no gates or locks."

Finally Jeremiah calls Elam to judgment. A particular, poignant irony here. Elam had been the last hope of the exiles. Perhaps, so speculation went, the Elamites could conquer Babylon and thus ensure the prompt end of their slavery.

Vain, a delusion. The prophet whose hopes so often come to naught is also a great dasher of false hopes. Jeremiah announces it; Elam is doomed. The proud nation of archers will be blown hither and yon like arrows in a hurricane. Its people will be scattered like a dust, exiles everywhere, at home nowhere. (Ezekiel is equally fierce: the warriors of Elam lie in the pit of the netherworld, slain in battle, an ossuary of the damned, a warning [32:24, 25].)

The drum of judgment beats on. In their bloody rise, pride of place, and bloodier fall, the empires are the unwitting instruments of—moral reality.

Thus, at one point, Babylon is (somewhat grudgingly) granted an approving title; the redoubtable empire is the blunderbuss of God: "My hammer, My weapon of war." At another, judgment falls on the adversary of peace and justice; "You will see Me repay Babylon and its people for all the evil they did to Jerusalem."

50:11–16 Because you revel in iniquity
>because rejoicing,
>>loud, lewd, derisive
>explodes, because
>your fortunes
>>lofty as Babel, deep
>as hell's stanchions, founded upon
>>ill fortune of My people—

>because you—
>pillager, warrior, spoliator
>stranger to mercy,
>harbinger of death, hearkening
>to self-inflation only—

>plunderer, incendiary!

>>in the fire
>yourself kindles,
>>>bodily
>>>I cast you
>>>My fury
>>>>never to be
>extinguished.

Remember: Empires Fall (51:50–64)

51:50–53. Remember, my people, the time of deliverance is near. A startlingly different emphasis. We have seen from the start (chap. 27) every promise of swift release from exile was scorned as false. A very bone of contention, Jeremiah urged the exiles to settle into their new land, to contribute to the common good; in effect, to forget.

A long time has passed; we near the end-time. And the message changes, as does the mood urged upon the people. Now—remember!

A note of Ecclesiastes: a time "for everything under the sun." A time to forget, a time to remember. Forget the false promises, the meretricious pseudo-prophets, the illusionists. Dismiss far from you everything that hinders, hobbles, haunts.

The forgetting is one with the "uprooting and pulling down, destroying and overthrowing," commended in the original grant of "authority over the nations." We have heard it in the text, as though it groaned from the very guts of Jeremiah. It is the "no" that must precede any truthful, heartfelt "yes."

Another question arises: What sort of authority can be his—an authority conferred by Yahweh, with considerable solemnity and seriousness, as we read? Conferred—and then in practice canceled, scorned, negated, put to naught, as the principalities conspire together, to make sport of, to overwhelm, the prophet, to kill him?

The question is haunting, perennial. Is such a delegation, its content and credential, more than a paper tiger in a storm?

This would seem to offer a clue: the authority of Jeremiah "over the nations" suffers the fate of the authority of Yahweh over the same entities. The authority is substantial, irresistible, universal, as declared in God's word. It is also utterly put to naught in practice, then and since; in the practice of war, international chicanery, domestic heartlessness.

And yet, the authority must be proclaimed, with this dire understanding: that the proclamation will be frustrated and held to mockery. Behold the "vocation to frustration" of the Jeremian kind.

And the later command: let the exiles now summon remembrance. It is one with the original "building and planting." One with the deliverance and return. These latter are the images that, as the book concludes, stand upon the page like a savior resurrected. All, despite all, shall be well.

The rhythms we have taken note of—a "no" prior to a "yes," yin and then yang—are one with the rhythms of Jeremiah's life: and by implication, of our own.

The same can hardly be said of the empires or their institutions, or for that matter, of those who help construct such, arm them, protect, validate, place their trust in them, batten off them, ensure their prospering. It goes without saying: the imperial nations grant no sense or logic to such commands as Jeremiah is charged with: "to uproot and to pull down, to destroy and to overthrow."

Why such violence, such profitless bravado? According to the common estimate of church and state, such institutions as the empire maintains—the "justice system," the economy, the military, the universities, the medical centers (yes, the death rows and abortion clinics)—all are self-validated, befit high culture, in point of fact function reasonably well.

Granted for sake of argument, this or that slight shortcoming in this or that respect. Be not set back, a bit more effort or will or skill, and all will be righted once more! (One calls to mind the fury of Yahweh at such persiflage, self-serving, oafish, blind of eye and heart—and one is set atremble: "For Yahweh hears the cry of the poor.")

Pull down, destroy?

The words are anathema; their proclamation is rife with danger (as Jeremiah discovered to his sorrow). Is this peevish fellow not talking anarchy, subversion, violence? Actions consequent to such dark urgings are hedged about sternly by law.

Nevertheless, we hearken to Jeremiah. He knows it in his bones (so do we). If a clear and courageous "no" is never uttered, a "yes" of substance is never spoken. Because no institution is condemned to be "uprooted and pulled down, destroyed and overthrown," the legitimizing of mass violence continues apace. (To be noted, in fear and trembling: after fifty years, the Pentagon, together with its subculture of legalized murder, is ever more firmly and extravagantly in place.)

The culture lurches along, burdened by an enormous military impedimenta, its bases and bombs and bombers and submarines and research labs and secret installations. "National security" is the mantra. One generation requires that such horrors be devised and set in place; willy-nilly another generation must inherit them.

For the present, for the indefinite future, in a weird vacuum of "no enemy," we pay and pay and amass and amass. The weapons proliferate; they stand as a kind of "second nature" within creation.

The moral implications the weapons once thrust at us like a gun barrel to the head, leave us numbed. So life goes; uphill all the way, blind fate and no vocation.

And shall one speak of a legacy to the children?—a polluted earth, a no-man's land, mined with danger and folly.

51:59–64. Another letter of Jeremiah is dispatched to the exiles (the first attempt to speak the truth of their situation is recounted in chap. 29). Now the "seventy years" near their close. A far different message is in order, and a different symbolic gesture. Seraiah the messenger is instructed to "see that you read all these words aloud" (New American Standard) "when you finish reading this book to the people" (Good News Bible).

(And we are offered the following as an [enlightened?] commentary on the text, which stated, one would think clearly, that the reading was to be "aloud," "to the people": "We presume that the reading has been done privately, for the divulgation of the oracle in Babylon would have been quite imprudent." And more, and worse. Extended oracles, comprising two chapters [50 and 51], have detailed the fall of Babylon. Now this for comment: "We will never know what was written in the book, and the redactor of the present narrative did not know either.")

The (public, no?) reading finished, to what effect we are not told, Seraiah is to attach the scroll to a rock and cast it in the Euphrates.

Revelation (18:21) tells of a like gesture, with added solemnity of detail; its protagonist is a "mighty angel," and the stone of Seraiah has wonderfully grown to a "large millstone." And instead of the river, the waters that receive the huge boulder are boundless, wild—"the sea."

Then to the gesture is added an angelic word of judgment: "This is how the great city of Babylon will be violently thrown down and will never be seen again" (Rev. 18:21).

Unlearn before learning. Years passed under a harsh Babylonian tutelage, seventy heavy years, yoke after yoke galling. Then to the eyes of Jeremiah's disciples and scribes a kind of predawn light appears, a hint on the horizon.

And another change of mood: the exiles must bestir themselves to hope, to a new exodus in the offing. The word of God, the blast of a shofar. Freedom now!

A campaign is underway; a momentous change of consciousness infects minds and hearts. It is as though "bones, dry bones" were knitting together in a desert place. Sleepers awaken; reality, reality! With divine sanction Babylon is fiercely set upon—as wicked, idolatrous, doomed.

The echoes of this outcry will reverberate in the Christian Bible as well; (in Revelation) Babylon, along with Rome, is portrayed as the icon and primal image of empire. Every form of wickedness and perversion is adduced: subjugation of foreigners, control of world markets and trade, their "dealing in slaves, even in human lives" (c.18, v.13).

Then the empire falls, collapses.

No recorded enemy is at the gates. The contradictions, animosities, and oppositions strain and stretch the imperial fabric; it falls in a rotten heap.

We note that Revelation need not correspond to what we know as "the facts." The biblical point is not to assemble the data of secular history, the how or why Babylon fell. The point is other: divine judgment on "empire as such."

This is how another, later amanuensis of how Yahweh viewed Babylon: "a woman seated on a red beast that had names insulting to God written all over it (Rev. 17:3), and so on, in like vein. Through such images of degradation, John of Patmos offers an "inner reading" of the dynamics of socialized pride, functioning outside all control or constraint.

Babylon: from the apex of glory under Nebuchadnezzar to utter collapse, and this in a matter of less than two decades!

And even this short passage of time must be syncopated, intensified, dramatized in Revelation. No cause or preamble is offered; we hear only a majestic angelic manifesto, "Fallen, fallen is Babylon the great!" (18:2).

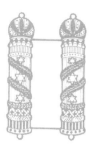

16
The King's Fate—
and Jeremiah's (52:1–34)

And finally, by way of closure, a later addition (reproducing 2 Kings 24:18–25). It is as though the awful days of defeat, destruction, and exile stand petrified in memory.

Jeremiah, his disciples, the author of Kings—it makes little difference. They return and return to those years, those seeming eons: drawing from the depths of memory images, events, humiliations beyond words, seeking in the welter what meaning may be cast upon present and future.

Another point: the repetition here of the passage from Kings must be accounted a matter of instruction. Our woebegone prophet! Is he to be vindicated at last?

The survivors are to know (so are we) that his detractors and persecutors were criminally guilty. See then: his prophecies stand like steles in a desert waste, sound and true.

A Noble Spirit (52:1–30)

52:1–11. The fate of Zedekiah is recounted straightforwardly, a kind of dying fall. The king's punishment is savage, plenary. He is captured, his sons executed before his eyes, his eyes plucked out. He dies in a Babylonian prison.

The account conveys much by indirection, even by omission. Whoever the author or editor, he would have us know that in Jeremiah there abides neither judgment nor mourning nor self-justification. Not a word of these, no emotional record; all such matters lie in other hands.

It is as though our prophet had attained the tranquillity and detachment of a bodhisattva. Polemic has yielded to silence.

He has seen all, undergone all, and withstood. Now he emerges into the light. He has become the light.

Best then, he would counsel, in the last years simply to set down the record, and live out one's allotted time. He is like a traveler in time, solitary. Companions one after another perish; he must bury them along the way, and trudge on.

52:12–16. We learn much here of the dark genius of the invader. Formerly, in rounding up captives, the net was cast wide—but with nice discrimination. The talented and prominent were dragged off. Once assimilated, they would serve well the interests of empire. In the third roundup recounted here, "the captain of the guard carried away...some of the poorest of the people, the rest of those who were left in the city, those who had deserted to the king of Babylon, and the rest of the artisans."

Before, a detritus was left behind, useful as slave labor on their own land. Now, the remnant of a remnant is left: "some of the poorest of the land, to be vinedressers and plowmen."

52:17–23. Memories, memories.

A veritable litany of loss is dwelt upon, loving, mournful, a final jeremiad, the last days of the city and the woe that followed. The invaders vandalously trash the temple, the heart of reality, and cart off the precious relics for booty.

Vulgarity is at work. Furnishings are weighed and disposed of, whether immense or minuscule no matter, precious or common, finely wrought or quotidian: "bronze columns,...carts,...shovels,...tools, ...bowls,...ash containers,...lamp stands..." It is as though the features, one by one, of a lost beloved were detailed, one by one, in mourning.

The temple of great Solomon is a rubble, the elite of the nation are seized, tortured, and killed.

Jeremiah dies in Egypt. Was he murdered there, by his own? This is the harsh, enduring gift of Yahweh. Nothing of grief or loss must be mitigated in his last days. Like Jesus, Jeremiah dies fully alive.

To such a point came this one, this voice and heart and passion, one of the noblest spirits to breathe mortal air.

A tragic life, a tragic ending?

Awful, yet befitting.

Jeremiah's Consolation: The Word Honored through All Time (52:31–34)

Out of this nettle, danger, pluck—a flower.

A note of hope and forgiveness concludes a life our Bible holds at heart. The king Jehoiachin had given the prophet small reason for affection or respect; quite the opposite. It was against this moody fainéant, it will be recalled, that Jeremiah aimed a scathing "woe" (22:13–17).

The indictment was fierce: it charged the ruler with extortion from the poor, extravagance at others' expense, even murder and oppression. (It was this same eminence, one remembers, who with scalding contempt cut the scroll of Jeremiah and, piece by piece, cast it in the fire, as it was read aloud to him. And after the episode, he sought the life of Jeremiah.)

We recall another tale: how the king disposed of a prophet Uriah, who had dared denounce him. All this by way of suggesting that without blame, Jeremiah could have ignored the fate of a constant tormentor. The prophet might even be thought (but the thought is beneath him) to take a bleak pleasure in the outcome; the king suffered the fate he wrought against others.

Nothing of this.

Jeremiah tells the story soberly, with a hint of approval for the magnanimity of the king of Babylon toward his adversary. Jehoiachin is released from prison; measures are taken, in view of comfort in his last days. The report of Jeremiah is endearingly detailed: "Evil-merodach treated him kindly.... Jehoiachin was permitted to change from his prison clothes and to dine at the king's table for the rest of his life. Each day for as long as he lived, he was given a regular allowance for his needs."

Had the king of the Jews, uncrowned and disenthroned, bowed with age and humiliation, undergone a change of heart? Fiery coals were heaped on an unworthy head. And not only by the king of Babylon. By Jeremiah, in the recounting.

Thus a final act dramatized the crowning irony of Jeremiah's life.

In the years of his troubled ministry, we saw how foreigners, castigated as idolaters and enemies by the chosen, dealt with him more benignly than his own. His besotted people stood firm against him, astonishingly, immorally consistent. Exile wrought no improvement whether in faith, hope, or charity.

Finis coronat opus: the end would crown and verify this life.

Can one speak of eventual consolation? Consolation to Jeremiah that his word, malevolently banished by contemporaries, should be rehabilitated and honored through all time, in all the world? Consolation that he should stand in the mind of the unborn, a biblical icon of the cost of uttering the word of God, of living by it? The suffering servant of our contempt?

It is as though his body was tattooed throughout with scenes of his own passion. As though thus pierced, a livid text emerged, and he a public show, a freak, a holy fool.

An illustrated man. As though he walked the world, displaying on his body a text: the bottomless plunge of our Fall, the scope of all but irretrievable loss and malice.

The Rules of the Fall.

First: no one is to live like this; it is decreed that no one is to live like this.

Further: the one who dares live like this will be harshly dealt with.

The average, so to speak, above all! Morality, nostrums, norms. If passionate about anything, then about this: that the tyranny of the average be maintained.

Does holiness venture into our world?

Suddenly that "average," somnolent, sleepily tolerant ("liberal," as is said, and "reformist") rears up, shows a fang. Someone has violated the average. The presence of such a one—worse, the consonant behavior—these summon a passion to crush that one.

The passionate throttling of an opposite number; dark be my light!

A story is hinted at by another, later scribe than Baruch; his named is Mark. He reports the word of another, greater prophet than Jeremiah. It may be of point here, as we finish this most bitter, but infinitely heartening, life.

The tale begins with a general statement, which grants access, perhaps, to a state of mind. Self-assurance, strength (possession, nine points of the law) once governed and guaranteed title to a certain property, a house. Those who dwelt there rejoiced in security of mind. They went about the ordinary business of the world, getting and spending, working, consuming, begetting perhaps. And in time, dying. The point of the story is not their fate, however; it concerns their claim. And a counterclaim.

If the claim remained indefinitely intact, there would be no story. This is the plain truth of the matter—no claim, no outcome. And yet hardly anyone (thus the story) sees or averts to—the worth or worthlessness of that claim. Let alone challenges it.

The property, according to our story, lies at the edge of the world. And yet it lies at the heart of the world.

What, one thinks, could be thought more typical, more uninteresting, more banal, than a cycle of routine governing the ebb and flow of those lives, those dwellers, apart, yet in our midst?

To each his own. Other have their own routine, similar to our protagonists; they too work and play, earn and spend, and eventually die.

Someone, however, shows an uncommon interest in observing the house and its inhabitants, their habitual comings and goings.

Let it be admitted that this mysterious observer is radically at odds with the tenants. The chief ingredient of the friction lies in this: he is convinced that the owners of the property are in fact interlopers, squatters. Their claim, however legitimated, to him is null and void. He has a counterclaim. The property belongs to himself, the observer.

But what of that "possession," that crucial "nine points," that "law" undeniably in the favor of the dwellers? He can point to nothing in the code of law that would even slightly favor himself.

No matter. Our claimant brushes all such difficulties aside.

Indeed he grants another meaning entirely to that term "possession" (and all that follows on it). He would have it thus: that the aforesaid inhabitants are themselves possessed, by this property. He takes note of jealousy and fear behind the eyes, fervent locks and bolts—yes, weapons in the house.

The situation comes to something more than expropriation. To this: those "owners" would have the whole world to resemble themselves. In pursuit of their "mission," they stir others to fear and dread. They would have everyone dwelling bolted and barred, one against the other, some against all.

A dark vision is theirs; it takes on the overtones of apocalypse: "...brother against brother, neighbor against neighbor. Rival cities will fight each other, rival kings will strive for power.... They will implore their idols for help, they will consult mediums and summon the spirits of the dead...."

Very few are aware of what is transpiring in the dwelling. Almost no one senses the atmosphere that issues from the house, what innuendoes and rumors and dark hints waft from it like a smoke—the way the world should be governed (and is not), how differently, darkly people should come to regard one another (and do not). Even to this point (eventually, gradually): who should flourish and who be denied place.

And ultimately, this: who is entitled to live, and who not.

The full irony of the situation: someone senses the atmosphere that broods over the dwelling, as well as the intent of the owners.

But of what use, this insight? Shall the observer raise a challenge to the dwellers and owners? But what chance has such a tactic before the law?

We are at an impasse.

The situation, if it rests there, allows for no story. The dwellers are in possession; according to the law their claim is intact.

Yet against all odds, and as a plain matter of history—the case did not rest there. The indictment reads like this: the outsider, against all conventional sense and unprovoked, "took the law into his own hands." He "broke and entered."

The owners were strong, the dwelling safe, the future unbreached. But he broke and entered, evicted the dark tribe, and so vacated their claim, abruptly, once for all.

Against all odds, through the courage of One, in persistence and risk, in the forging of a new claim and covenant, we had our story.

We began, in virtue of that act of his, to—exist.

Deus Concedat Victoriam
Doxe to Theo Panton Heneka